The Franklin Library Association

Building the Future of the Nation's First Public Library

Franklin Public Library, Paul Vicarrio

A Historical Research Project of the Trustees of the Franklin Library Association:

Elegy

I pause to make an offering here,
A poet's tribute at the bier
Of one who trod the ways of truth.
The source of strength to man and youth.
Horace Mann, thy honored name
Throughout the world is known to fame.
The trophies of thy matchless mind
In all the world a lodgment find.
For wisdom, moral force and power
A line of names appear this hour.
Fair products of New England soil
In art, and science, and in toil.
Thurston, Fisher, Metcalf, Thayer,
Gilmore, Rockwood, Bullard, Ware.
Adams, Daniels, Whiting, Dean,
Kingsbury, Clark, Ray, Pond, and Greene.
Richardson and Bacon too,
Nason, Woodward, Blake, Ballou.
Other names I too do find,
Kind in heart and rich in mind.

-- Extract from *Ode to Franklin*,
published with a volume of verse titled
"*Pastoral Summer - Franklin*"
by Wallace Ruthven Richardson, 1882

The Franklin Library Association:
Building the Future of the Nation's First Public Library

Eamon McCarthy Earls & Alan R. Earls –Consulting Editors:

Dedication

This book is intended to serve not only as a history of the Franklin Library Association and its role in preserving, protecting, and enhancing the legacy of Benjamin Franklin, but also as a testament to many particularly public-spirited individuals. These are individuals who have gone "above and beyond" through their extensive commitment of time and energy in furthering the worthy goals of the association; some – notably the members of the Ray family -- have been able to supplement that commitment with extraordinary financial generosity, as well. There has also been a long line of members who have advocated, preserved, and contributed to fulfilling the mission of the association throughout the decades. Although not inclusive, the following individuals were especially instrumental at key points in the history of the Association and are included in this dedication: Elizabeth Brunelli, Howard Warcup, Anne L. Whelan, Henry Freniere, Clara M. Lodi, Elynor Crothers, and Nancy J. Rappa.

The newly renovated library and its history room are their monument; this tome, along with the Historical Room at the library, which they helped fund, a lasting memorial.

Acknowledgements

This history of the Franklin Library Association would not be possible without the dedicated staff, faithful patrons and tenacious members of the Association who have spearheaded the work of supporting the Franklin Public Library through more than a century and a half. Within the professional library community, the Association wishes to thank Vicki Buchanio Earls, long-time reference librarian, for her tireless work to preserve and arrange the Association's historical resources—and those of the library and the town—in a form that ensures their continuation into the future and accessibility for generations to come. As the library's guide during this time of growth and change, the Association also wishes to thank Library Director, Felicia Oti, for her continued work with the Association.

Above, the final annual meeting of the Franklin Library Association, Nov. 15, 2022. Left to right, Nancy J. Rappa, Beth Mucciarone, Greg Dellorco, Edward Padden, Shirley Borruso, Joan McGuire, and Scott Nolan and Armand Fernandez behind McGuire.

Table of Contents

Chapter 1: Exeter or Franklin?

In October of 1986, the American Library Association's Library Journal confirmed what most residents of Franklin, Massachusetts, already believed: The Franklin Public Library is the oldest free town lending library in America. It earned this distinction, according to the Journal, because it was "created by the Townspeople and open to all on an equitable basis," and it was "managed as a public trust."

Of course, that only tells a tiny part of the remarkable story of the Franklin Public Library, its creation and fortuitous preservation, as well as its growth and maturation under the wise and generous stewardship of a small group of citizens: The Franklin Library Association.

As we become more accustomed to the thriving city of Franklin that seems so familiar in the early 21st century, and the outstanding library resources to which the community has access, it can be easy to forget the distant, humble origins of the town that we call home. Local history is rarely a component in high school history classes and many modern residents of Franklin hail from around the region, the US and the world, so it can be easy to disregard our town's collective past.

The Franklin Library Association, and later the closely allied Ray Memorial Association, grew up in a community that would change and reinvent itself many times throughout the existence of the organizations. What began as a sleepy farming hamlet later transformed into a booming mill town, an exurb and later a suburb of Boston that today has become a city of highways, industrial parks, greenspaces, neighborhoods, and information technology. Without the substantial input of local business and strong community, an organization like the Franklin Library Association would have faltered and died. But how did the community of today come to be?

Answers to such questions are never simple, but they lie rooted in the colonial history of Massachusetts. Nearly 400 years ago, in 1630, Puritan ships sailing from England lowered their anchors for the first time off of Massachusetts. Within a few short months, the settlers, whose creed would later come to be known as Congregationalism, had established the Massachusetts Bay Colony. Founded as a more distant result of Gutenberg's printing press and the Protestant Reformation, the Puritan communities of Massachusetts possessed a highly educated population with substantial love of the written word. Most of the paper in the colony's books—and even the books themselves—originated in England and were shipped to New England, making them especially expensive. Nevertheless, these Puritan communities placed great emphasis on learning—particularly the teachings of the Bible which they abided by strictly.

And, while early settlements may have lacked a formal library, the settlers brought copies of their trusted family Bibles along with them so that they could review scripture and they shared religious tracts among themselves.

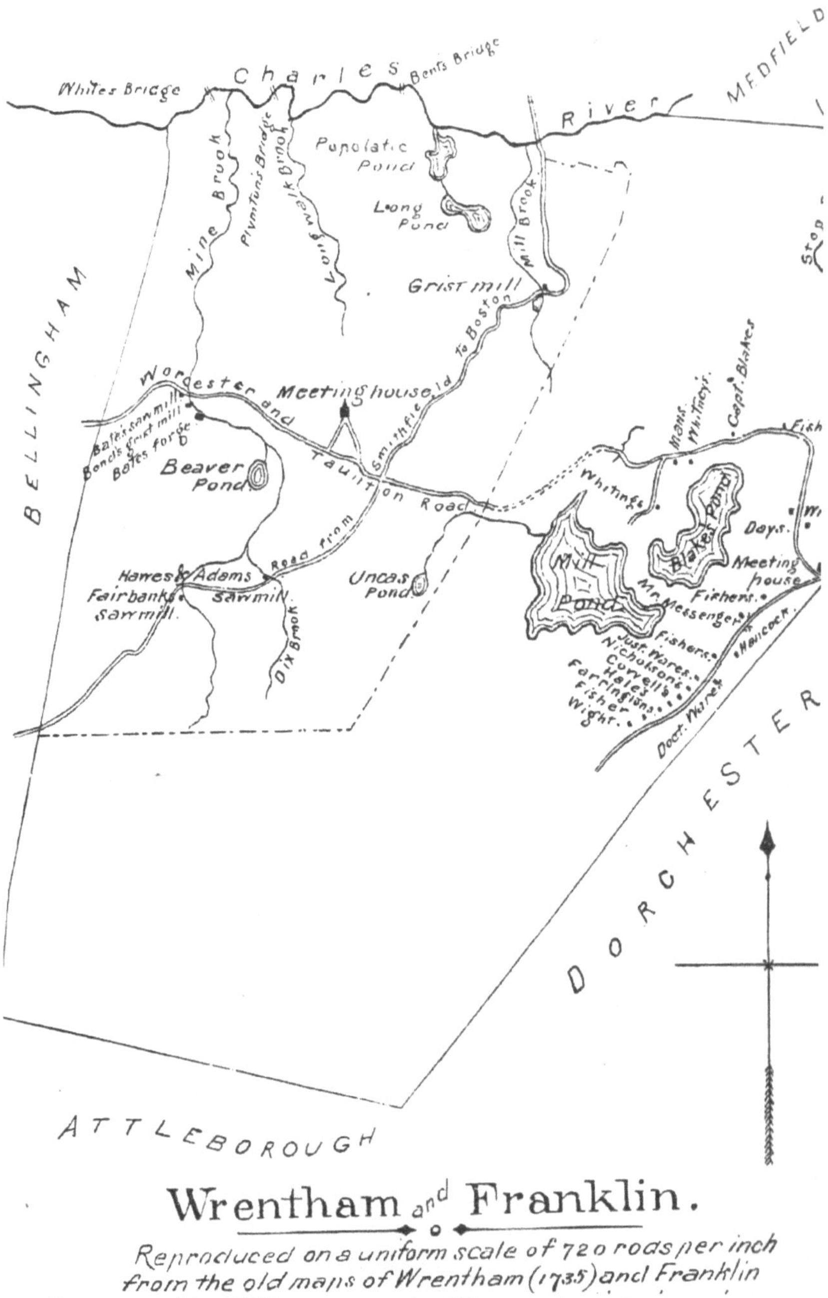

Franklin as it appeared in 1796 was a much different place than today. A population of a few thousand farmers spread across an area including parts of modern-day Norfolk, coalescing into a community at the Meeting House by the town common.

Early on, settlers planted crops, homes, and families in communities that would come to be known as Charlestown, Salem and Boston. If worse came to worse, they had access to the sea for trading—or escape—thanks to expansive natural harbors. As coastal settlements gained stability and began to prosper, thousands more settlers poured into New England, setting up communities farther inland.

A royal charter granted them the land from the Plymouth Colony in the south to the Merrimack River in the north. Thus, besides Boston, most of the settlements were situated to the north and to the west of the meandering Charles River. Scattered amongst those north of the river, were communities like Newtowne (today known as Cambridge), Watertown, and even Concord which would gain its fame later on in the Revolutionary War. Very soon, settlers also began to migrate to the region southwest of Boston. They sought to fill a frontier, where few European settlers had ventured permanently, beside those of the infant Plymouth Colony itself.

By 1635, the settlers south of the Charles had concocted a permanent community of their own and were officially recognized by the General Court.

The new "plantation" – as large agricultural settlements were termed – was originally dubbed Contentment, covering about 200 square miles of land that had an earlier point in the colony's history been granted to Newtowne. This 1600s plantation spanned most of modern-day Norfolk County, to the border with current day Bristol County, which was then the frontier of the Plymouth Colony.

The first few hundred daring individuals made their home only a few miles from Boston in Contentment's center. Recalling place names from England, the settlers renamed the plantation almost immediately to become the town Dedham.

With the arrival of the 1660s, Dedham center had begun to outstrip its local resources leading some community members to consider resettlement. Simultaneously, tales of deposits of metals like copper further inland began to circulate. It seemed that vast western meadowland where these rumors were centered might serve as the basis for both a new industry and a fresh start.

But before the first wave of committed settlers could leave, the Dedham selectmen ordered a survey of the western extent of the plantation. Whatever they discovered seems to have confirmed their hopes. Western Dedham was worthy of settlement. And there was reliable fresh water and fishing in ponds such the one we now call Lake Pearl, just south of Franklin.

In spite of the confirmation from the surveyors, the town fathers remained anxious; the "frontier" was too far away from Dedham proper making it potentially vulnerable to Indian attack.

At the time that Dedham was setting up a western settlement, Metacom---better known as King Philip—succeeded his father, Massasoit, as leader of the Wampanoags. The rapid growth of European settlement and increasing marginalization of native inhabitants had begun to undermine the friendly relations of the two communities, long embodied in the person of Massasoit. Despite these concerns, settlers from Dedham finalized plans for their new plantation and settled the land near Lake Pearl. The new community was known as Wollomonopoag (present day Wrentham). Within a few years of settlement 34 lots had been created out of the community's central 600-acre plot, as well as a 'cow-common,' where the settlers' livestock could graze communally.

During the first five years of 1670s, Wollomonopoag hired a minister and recruited a blacksmith, constructed a small grist mill to grind farmers' grain, and took further steps toward independence from Dedham. So successful was the community that the General Court incorporated the Town of Wrentham (including the area that is today Franklin) on October 17, 1673. It was a town, to be sure, but one with few frills. Education, books, and libraries were for the future.

However, almost before the ink was dry on the charter for the new town of Wrentham, it was nearly wiped from the face of the earth by a cataclysmic event masterminded by the former owners of the town's land--King Philip and the Wampanoags. In 1675, three Wampanoags, possibly acting on behalf of King Philip, were arrested and hanged in Plymouth for the murder of a Native American who had converted to Christianity. The hanging was regarded as an affront by the Wampanoag tribe.

Fighting was quick to break out, and although no single group had declared war, violence quickly escalated—King Philip's War had begun.

King Philip's War came like a bolt from the blue. Town after town went up in smoke. King Philip's warriors and his allies were remarkably successful, sweeping down to snuff out settlement after settlement, especially along the frontier, destroying towns like Springfield, Hadley, and Lancaster. But even long-settled communities near the coast were not immune. Settlers in Wrentham could see the writing on the wall. Living in isolation from larger communities, the town and its inhabitants might not survive an attack. Rather than wait around for enemy warriors to arrive, the settlers loaded their animals with provisions and hastened women and children to the comparative safety of Dedham.

However, after long months of bloody give and take, the European settlers gradually regained the initiative. The war cost the Indians more than the English. Six hundred settlers were dead across the region, but the Indians had lost three thousand of their number. Back in Dedham once again, the Wrentham settlers were left wondering about the future of their town. The settlers ultimately voted to return and rebuild Wrentham from the ground up. Ten years after the war, in 1685, the town premiered a new meetinghouse and set aside 25 acres for a school. New townspeople were also arriving from Medfield and settling in the northwest part of town.

By the 1700s the new village on Mine Brook, was generating much of the Wrentham's business. Two sawmills churned out boards, cattle grazed in the moist lowlands, and on higher ground corn stalks took root. Residents were still subject to Wrentham's laws, including an implicit requirement to attend church each week miles away in Wrentham proper. But some felt that distance and their growing population should lead to independence from the rest of the town. Settled so far from the Wrentham church, some settlers sought to join Medway, where the meeting house was easier to reach.

Among the most prominent malcontents was John Pond. After many years, in 1737 the General Court finally took notice of Pond and his supporters and sent a committee to investigate the matter. The committee recommended generally in favor of autonomy for the northwestern residents. The new second precinct (the future town of Franklin) was large, a rectangle four and a half miles wide, and six and a half miles from north to south. Before long, the new precinct had its own meeting house, a first step toward municipal life.

When the American Revolution began, the preparation of volunteer militias led communities to push again for greater independence. The second precinct petitioned Wrentham to become a separate town in 1777 and the General Court approved the petition in 1778. A new group of selectmen went to work coming up with a name for their new town. The first name they chose was Exeter. In fact, in founding documents, the town name was written in as Exeter, Massachusetts. But at the last moment, the selectmen had a change of heart, scratching out Exeter and replacing it with Franklin, in honor of the famed American statesman and Boston native, Benjamin Franklin.

It was a good name for a town in open rebellion against Britain, and sounded more American than Exeter.

Franklin—a new town with a new government — had plenty of work to get done, including approval of a new Massachusetts constitution authored by John Adams, and managing its finances at a time when paper money was rapidly shrinking in value and little of the older colonial currency was available.

The choice of the name would also prove fortuitous in leading the community to become America's "library town."

This preserved 1600s home in Medfield, Massachusetts closely resembles the homes typical of early Wrentham settlers as the 2nd Precinct (the future Franklin) was being settled.

Chapter 2: The Gift

Statue of Benjamin Franklin at the Ray Memorial Library Building.

Four years after the American Revolution ended, news from the United States began to travel across the Atlantic Ocean once again. In Paris, Benjamin Franklin heard, for the first time, that a town had been named in his honor. In local lore, it was at this point that the new town asked Franklin for a meetinghouse bell. Never one to disappoint, Franklin did give the town a gift, but not the one that the selectmen had hoped for. In place of a bell, Franklin sent his famous gift of books, believing that future generations would be, "More fond of sense than sound."

One of Franklin's colleagues in England, Dr. Price, bought up books and sent them by ship to

Massachusetts. The original gift of 116 books[1] went over well with the town, and the community decided to buy an additional 100 volumes. The collection featured famous 18th century philosophers such as Locke and Montesquieu.

Libraries were by no means a novelty in the region or in the English colonies. In fact, neighboring Wrentham had one of the earliest parish lending libraries in the colonies, and had served as temporary home for Brown University's books during the Revolution. Franklin himself established a library in Philadelphia and the Redwood Library and Athenaeum, a private subscription library in Newport, Rhode Island, had started in 1747. But a town library was something new.

At first, the Town of Franklin modeled its collection after Wrentham's, open only to members of the local parish (which included almost everyone in town). However, in 1788, the selectmen decided to go a step further and make the library available to *everyone*, marking the start of the first true public library in the United States. However, books alone did not a library make. Books needed to be stored somewhere and someone needed to be in charge. Both problems were solved, for a time at least with the appointment by the town of the first librarian, Dr. Nathanael Emmons, a famous Congregationalist minister and theologian appointed to the local parish in 1773. He proved to be a careful but controversial steward.

Though lacking the hoped-for bell, the town built a new meetinghouse in the 1780s, and the community, especially in Unionville, began to see a growth in business. Although its grazing land and bog iron helped to bring in some money, Unionville appears to have been one of the poorest areas in the town's early years due to its poor cropland. In 1782, Timothy Rockwood began to change that image, opening the town's first apothecary and a grocery store to serve the village. In 1800, Nathaniel Thayer and his family moved to Unionville, and started out in manufacturing alongside the Makepeaces and Rockwoods. Two Thayer men, Davis and Asa moved to Franklin Center and set up a straw products business. With money from that venture, Asa started the Franklin Hotel, by the common, one of the first inns in town.

About the same time, Horace Mann was born on May 4, 1796, at the family farm at the Four Corners, an intersection of two major roads, known today as Central Street (Route 140) and King Street. The Mann homestead was located where the Horace Mann Plaza is today. In the 1790s, it was known as the Mann Plain because of the land's general flatness. The family owned a two-story house, heated in winter by a central chimney, and surrounded by outbuildings for livestock.

Horace's parents were strict and reserved, even harsh, but they instilled their son with strong morals from a young age. The Four Corners, the Mann family's strategic location helped to broaden Horace's world view—on one occasion, a young woman visited the family, displaying tremendous skill in Latin recitation that inspired his lifelong interest in the language.

---

[1] See appendix for list and description.

Horace was an eager learner, but until the age of 15 he had only a few weeks of formal schooling, though he was far from being an illiterate bumpkin. Much of what he learned as a young man came from Benjamin Franklin's donated books. Although he devoured almost all the books in the library, he later looked back on the experience with regret. "I wasted my youthful ardor upon its martial pages, and learned to glory in war, which both reason and conscience have since taught me to consider almost universally a crime. Oh! When will men learn to redeem that childhood in their offspring which was lost to themselves?"

By nature, Horace Mann seems to have been a gentle person, but his deep dislike for Dr. Emmons was legendary. His 12-year-old brother, James Mann, drowned in Uncas Pond on a Sunday, while swimming instead of attending church service. According to a Mann biographer, the death of James Mann—and the events of his funeral would haunt Horace for the rest of his life.

Far from exhibiting sympathy toward the family or sorrow at the death of the young man, Dr. Emmons found in the incident grounds for criticizing the deceased at his own funeral. In essence, he told the Mann family that their son had deserved to drown for skipping church on the Sabbath. The event left lasting scars. According to one of Horace Mann's lifelong friends (as related in a 1904 biography), "He [Horace Mann] said he [James Mann] was a charming boy, and that his death immediately brought home to his heart the terribleness of the theological views in which he was educated... A strange fascination would impel him, Sunday after Saturday, to find in Watt's hymn book, and read over and over again, a certain verse, which must be eliminated in modern editions, for I cannot find it; but it depicted the desolation of a solitary soul in eternity, rudderless and homeless."

"He thought he could see in his mother's face a despair beyond the grief of losing the mortal life of her son; and when, at the funeral, Dr. Emmons, instead of suggesting a thought of consoling character, improved the opportunity to address a crowd of young persons present on the topic of 'dying unconverted,' and he heard his mother groan, a crisis took place in his experience..."

Dr. Emmons the figure at the center of it all was controversial and described with bitterness in Mann's later writing: "More than toil, or by privation of any natural taste, was the inward joy of my youth blighted by theological inculcations. The pastor of the church in Franklin was the somewhat celebrated Dr. Emmons, who not only preached to his people, but ruled them for more than fifty years. He was an extreme Calvinist—a brilliant but often extremely unkind person. He expounded the doctrines of total depravity, election and reprobation, and not only the eternity, but the extremity, of hell torments, unflinchingly and in their most terrible significance; while he rarely if ever descanted upon the joys of heaven, and never, to my recollection, upon the essential and necessary happiness of a virtuous life."

However, even in death Dr. Emmons had as many admirers as detractors. Duane Hamilton

Hurd (in his 1884 history of Norfolk County), wrote that, "In one aspect Dr. Emmons has been and still is misrepresented. He was not curt, dogmatic, and repellent. He was not unsocial and austere to his people, nor a bugbear to the young. He was affable, genial, and witty, and enjoyed a good joke as keenly as anyone." However, for many people, such as Horace Mann, the only alternative to Dr. Emmons and his strict Congregationalist faith was conversion to Unitarianism or Universalism— two sects gaining converts from New Englanders tired of the strict faith of their forefathers.

Reverend Jacob Ide (grandson of Dr. Emmons, who spoke at the town centennial in 1878) said of his famous grandfather, "...I suppose that I am placed here as a relic of Dr. Emmons' ministry and am expected to represent it by contrast. I hoped that Edison would have perfected his phonograph so that it could be placed on Dr. Emmons' tombstone and he could have spoken for himself. I confess, sir, that I am proud of my grandfather; but I am afraid, if he were here to-day, that he would not be willing to reciprocate the compliment...Dr. Emmons' ministry must certainly be regarded as a successful ministry, for he made his people do as he pleased...Men carried home from the sanctuary [church] something that was not only worth remembering, but something that was not easy to forget."

Emmons was not an easy man to forget, it seems, and with good reason. He spent 54 years as Franklin's minister, until his death in 1827, running the public library out of his barn, as a sort of sideline. And his demise left the library in limbo; a municipal puzzle that would not begin to be solved for a generation.

Shown here in an 1870s lithograph, Dr. Nathaneal Emmons' house was a prominent landmark in downtown Franklin up until the 1860s. The famous—and controversial—preacher owned the land which later became Dean College and served as the town's first librarian.

In the meantime, though the library's first great student, Horace Mann, had already left town, destined to have an impact on the world far beyond that of even Emmons himself.

After leaving Franklin, Horace Mann studied at Brown University and was admitted to the bar as an attorney. But the world had more in store for Mann than life as a village lawyer. After joining the Unitarian faith, Horace Mann gathered up local supporters and ran for office,

Horace Mann—one of the first to profit by Franklin's gift of books.

representing Dedham in the General Court. Mann rose quickly through the ranks of state government, becoming president of the Massachusetts Senate. But he wasn't content to simply legislate along conventional pathways.

Along with Dorothea Dix and other reformers, Mann created the state's first insane asylum in Worcester, ending the cruel treatment and jailing of people with mental illness.

In the 1830s, Mann was named the head of the newly created Massachusetts Board of Education. As a child, he himself had been unable to attend school, and he had paid his way through Brown University by braiding straw hats. He believed that free, standardized, public education was essential to society's future. Studying the public education system of the German kingdom, Prussia, Mann created a plan for Massachusetts[2]. In his new plan, 'normal' schools would train teachers in modern methods of teaching that involved fewer beatings and more lessons for students. Students were also required to attend school up until a certain age. The first normal schools (present day state universities) were soon opened in Bridgewater and Framingham. To normalize schooling, Mann planned to implement standardized testing and standard curriculums.

Massachusetts congressman (and former president) John Quincy Adams died in 1848, and Mann was voted in to replace him. In Washington, Mann represented the anti-slavery initiatives of the Whig Party. The capital buzzed with debate about slavery, leaving Mann exhausted. In 1852 he returned to Massachusetts to run as an anti-slavery candidate for governor. Losing the race, he was appointed president of Antioch College in Ohio. Mann passed away in 1859, and was buried in Providence, but his educational system lived on and spread across the country. And he left us his appreciation of libraries born of his early acquaintance with the dusty tomes in Dr. Emmons' barn: "Had I the power, I would scatter libraries over the whole land, as the sower sows his wheat-field."

[2] From early colonial times, many New England towns had informal public schools, supported by the local government, but these schools varied greatly in what they taught, and access to education was still limited.

Mann Statue facing Emmons Street, Paul Vicario, photographer

Chapter 3: Forming the Association: 1858-1880

With the death of Reverend Emmons, the "problem" of what to do with Franklin's donation and Emmons' own acquisitions remained unresolved. The books apparently led a peripatetic existence stored here and there and at best treated to benign neglect. But changes were on the horizon.

By the late 1850s, southern New England was an up and coming landscape of small farm hamlets with growing numbers of mills, linked by the first generation of wood-fired locomotives traveling on fragile iron rails. Small towns were no longer isolated. It was an age of improvements – and libraries were much in discussion.

By 1858, the *Milford Journal*—a predecessor of the *Milford Daily News*—had begun to record the first rumblings of a library association in that community. During the muggy summer of 1858, on June 26, the Journal printed its Saturday morning run. The front page of the newspaper was adorned with the Journal's slogan written in Gothic script: "A family journal of useful knowledge, literature, science, art, agriculture and general intelligence," with a second subhead labeling the Journal as 'independent.'

The front page was occupied by the usual seven columns of text. Included were 'business cards,' for various local businesses, including M. Harris furniture and carpeting and Clement, Colburn & Co. advertising their boots and shoes. Charles Swain chipped in a poem about the arrival of summer, while the right-hand column was occupied by "A Lesson for a Christian," about Babylon, written in flowery words. Much of the front-page was occupied with miscellaneous news and commentary, including "Mrs. Skiddy gets a bargain," an item about a "roguish" woman arrested in Lowell for "larceny of clothing," and the discovery of gold in Iowa.

Looking past all the local color, perhaps the most important news story of the day was hidden on a different page, under the heading, "Particular attention to this notice is requested—Public library for Milford."

"The citizens of this town, interested in forming a public library to meet the wants of this community, are earnestly invited to be present at an adjourned meeting to be held at Washington Hall, No. 4, next Wednesday evening at 8 o'clock. A large meeting of those interested in establishing such an institution is vital to the enterprise. Reader, let not such a noble project fall for want of your presence."

Milford was not alone. Those middle years of the 19th century saw libraries increasingly as necessities for even the smallest of town.

Yet, Franklin was already among the fortunate. An anonymous letter (cryptically signed with the letter T) published in the *Traveler* newspaper in Boston, March 4, 1858, lay down the gauntlet:

"At the time this Library was presented, the town added thereto about the same number of volumes, in which were included several works by Dr. Franklin himself, and which his modesty forbade him to number in his gift. Since that time not a volume has been added, except certain public documents from the State or National Government. For some years past the Library has been neglected to a degree that is really dishonorable to the town. Some of the volumes are missing, and very few people appear to set much value upon it, either for the sake of the books, or as a gift from Dr. Franklin. It is lamentable that it is so. If some towns possessed it, they would rear a beautiful edifice, in which the books might be preserved, and make it the nucleus of a large collection of works. We hope it will yet be so here. In private circles, the matter is the theme of conversation to some extent, and we trust that soon we shall wipe away the disgrace of treating this sacred gift with such neglect."

As the letter hinted, those "private circles" were at work making 1858 the year in which several interested parties launched the Franklin Library Association. For much of Franklin's existence, until recent decades, Milford, Attleborough and Woonsocket were the nearest large towns or cities and together, they split a local monopoly on Franklin's news that wouldn't be broken until the early 1870s, with the establishment of Franklin's first town newspaper.

Fortunately, the history of the Franklin Library Association is not entirely silent for the 1850s. Town reports from the early 1870s help to describe the origins of the Association shortly before the Civil War.

`Not long after Milford's meeting, a group of Franklin citizens including Joseph Gordon Ray, of whom more will be heard, gathered with a similar purpose, in December, 1858. "...the citizens of Franklin, feeling the necessity of providing suitable reading matter for those who had time and a desire to avail themselves of the privileges of a library, met together and adopted a plan to form an association for that purpose."

The leading figure in the Association, often believed to have been the source of the letter in the *Traveler*, Rev. William Makepeace Thayer, a well-known author, was particularly concerned about the original Franklin books, calling them "among the almost forgotten things of this town." Apparently, no one objected to that characterization and in 1859, the Town voted to put the collection in the hands of the Association.[i]

Initially, as winter winds swept into Franklin, the Association's founder sought to create a private library, operating in the public interest that would finance itself through a combination of subscriptions, fines, and donations. With a lack of public funding, such an arrangement was the only way at the time to build a feasible public library, that could go beyond the bookshelves-amidst-the straw in Dr. Emmons' barn.

REV. WILLIAM M. THAYER.

"With that in view, and with a determination to accomplish the objects desired, those of our citizens who had the requisite means subscribed to a common fund very liberally, many of whom subscribed each the sum of one hundred dollars." A hundred dollars was a substantial contribution in 1858—in 2019 dollars, that comes out to something like 3,000 dollars a head. From that time, through the tumult of the Civil War and beyond, the Association maintained its oversight, though in 1871, the town briefly reclaimed its inheritance.

After the Franklin Library Association trustees submitted their report, the Franklin selectmen, "voted to place the care and custody," of the Franklin Library's entire collection in the hands of the Association. The agreement stated that the town's library books would be kept with the Association's books, "for the free use of the citizens of the Town, subject to proper rules and regulations." The agreement would remain in force, "until otherwise ordered by a vote of the Town." In addition to this landmark agreement, the selectmen, convening in the meeting house on West Central Street (which has housed the Historical Commission's Franklin Historical Museum since 2010) made another decision to benefit the library; they agreed to chip in an additional $161.16 from the town treasury, $150 would go directly to the Franklin Library Association. The Association could thank the generosity of the selectman, but they had, in a sense, "gone to the dogs" – allocating the sum from the town treasury that had come from dog license fees within the town. Underscoring its long-term commitment and ambition, the Association began to explore formal incorporation at this time.

The 1872 town report cited other forms of generosity from the town and allied thinking between both groups. For instance, after contributing the money from dog licenses, the town went ahead and agreed that, "the Directors of said Association are authorized to draw on the Town Treasury for such sums as may be needed, not to exceed the above amount, and in consideration of the grants made to the Association." In other words, the Association's Director would have a special privilege to request funds from the town to support the town's role in the library, whether from dog license fees or others sources of money, so long as the request did not exceed the original town grant.

To guarantee that the Franklin Library Association was upholding its important new role, the town stated that the, "Directors are requested to make a report annually to the Town, stating in detail the expenditures and any other items of general interest pertaining to the Association." The report would be 'furnished' seasonally to the town's auditor, so that he would be able to include it in his report of receipts and local expenses. At the time, Franklin held its annual meeting in March—the final deadline for all submissions by the Association.

October 2 of that same year also saw the Association formally incorporated under the laws of the Commonwealth, with the words: *Be it known that Henry M. Greene, Joseph G. Ray, Alpheus A. Russegue, A.E. Daniels, D. Thayer Jr., F.B. Ray, E.E. Baker, and James M. Freeman have associated themselves with the intention of forming a corporation under the name Franklin Library Association...*

Baker (Erastus Emmons), born July 28, 1825, was noted for having been the clerk of the First Congregational Church for some 25 years.
Freeman, as of the 1880 census, was a small-scale shoe manufacturer, employing up-to 25 people. He later served as Franklin Postmaster, was a town selectman and treasurer, and was on the Massachusetts Board of Railroad Commissioners.
Greene, was an attorney in town and a selectman.
Ray, (F.B.), a shoddy (cloth) manufacturer.
Ray, (Joseph G.), also a shoddy manufacturer.
Russegue, among other duties, served as town clerk and had been a state representative.
Thayer, (Davis, Jr.) was president of the Benjamin Franklin Savings Bank.

The very next year, the town again voted to place the care of its books in the hands of the Association.[ii]

These were years of building in Franklin, and the Franklin Library Association was not the only source of improving activities. In fact, an equally momentous activity had been under contemplation on the educational front involving some of the same interested citizens. In addition to its agricultural and industrial output, New England was second to none in higher education, turning out more college graduates (still mostly teachers or ministers) than almost any other part of the country. Indeed, most colleges began affiliated with a religious sect. Joining the fray, in 1852, Universalists founded a college in Medford on land donated by

Charles Tufts. (Some sources indicate that Franklin was originally considered as a location for the college.)

With an eye to the future, the Universalists set up a committee to create yet another new institution of higher education – a preparatory school that would lead students toward eventual enrollment at Tufts.

As the committee solicited contributions of land and money, Stoughton was the first community to reply. Stoughton Universalists were willing to offer 20,000 dollars and a site to build a college. However, Stoughton was outdone by Oliver Dean in Franklin. Dean was one of the wealthiest and most respected men in town. He owned Dr. Emmons' former estate (in Franklin Center) and offered the Universalists 60,000 dollars and nine acres. In 1864 the committee accepted Dean's princely offer.

Trustees were soon appointed, a charter was secured, and the groundbreaking took place in 1866. In 1867, the cornerstone was laid. Because of the economic problems that followed the Civil War the cost of building materials and workers rose rapidly, so that Oliver Dean eventually paid out 75,000 dollars for construction. The building was completed in 1868 and Dean Academy was born. The newly finished school was very modern, equipped with brand new furniture and a 'gas apparatus,' for lighting. The new school, Dean Academy, was a source of immense pride for the local Universalist congregation. Out of all the towns in Massachusetts, many with larger numbers of Universalists than Franklin, their town had been given a great distinction.

The original Dean Hall as it appeared in the late 1860s.

Facsimile of Association Incorporation Document

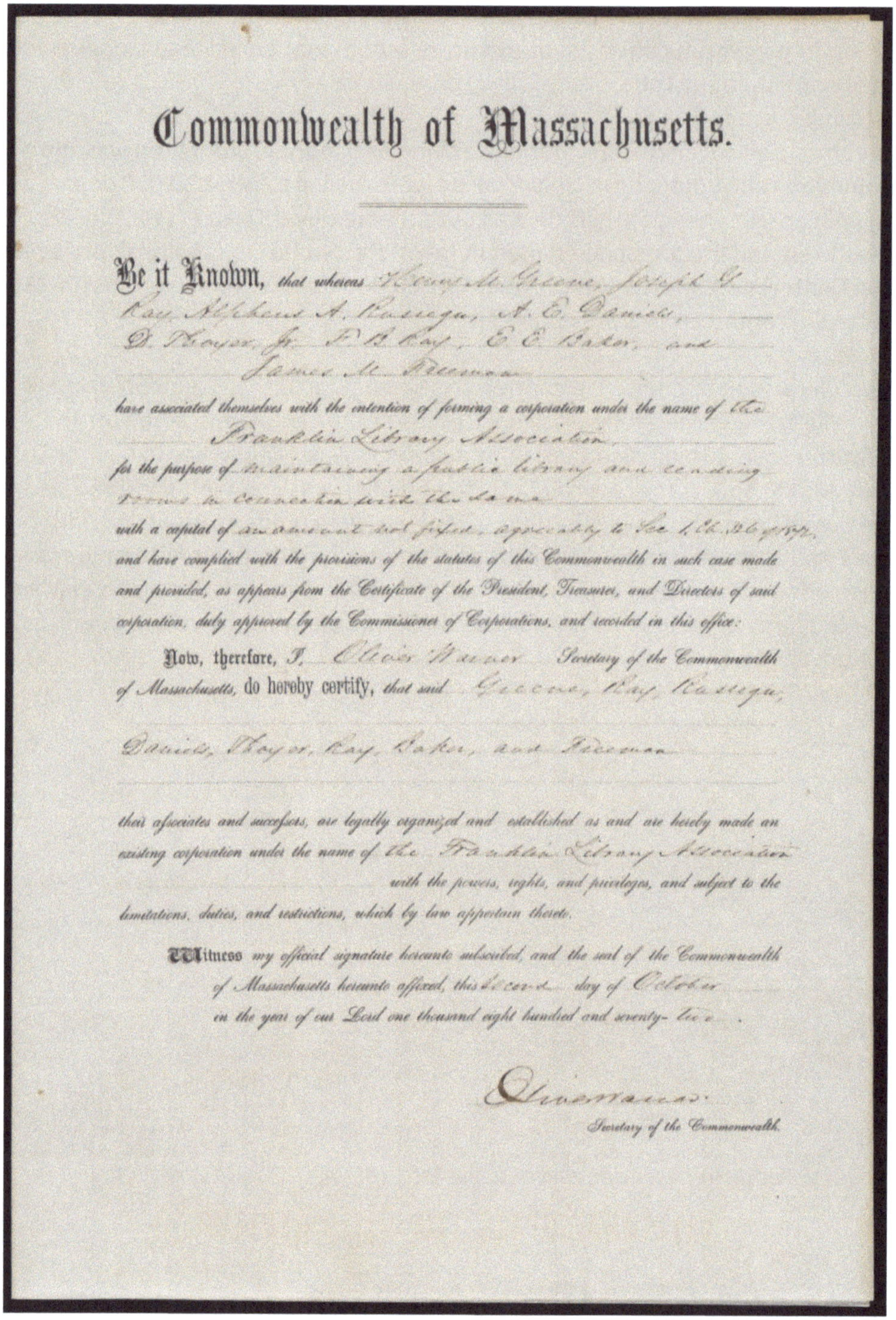

Commonwealth of Massachusetts.

Be it Known, that whereas Henry M. Greene, Joseph G. Ray, Alpheus A. Russegue, A. E. Daniels, D. Thayer, Jr. F. B. Ray, E. E. Baker, and James M. Freeman

have associated themselves with the intention of forming a corporation under the name of the Franklin Library Association

for the purpose of maintaining a public library and reading rooms in connection with the same

with a capital of an amount not fixed, agreeably to Sec 1. Ch. 36 of 1872, and have complied with the provisions of the statutes of this Commonwealth in such case made and provided, as appears from the Certificate of the President, Treasurer, and Directors of said corporation, duly approved by the Commissioner of Corporations, and recorded in this office:

Now, therefore, I, Oliver Warner Secretary of the Commonwealth of Massachusetts, do hereby certify, that said Greene, Ray, Russegue, Daniels, Thayer, Ray, Baker, and Freeman

their associates and successors, are legally organized and established as and are hereby made an existing corporation under the name of the Franklin Library Association with the powers, rights, and privileges, and subject to the limitations, duties, and restrictions, which by law appertain thereto.

Witness my official signature hereunto subscribed, and the seal of the Commonwealth of Massachusetts hereunto affixed, this second day of October in the year of our Lord one thousand eight hundred and seventy-two.

Oliver Warner

Secretary of the Commonwealth.

In addition to his largesse in support of Dean Academy, Oliver Dean's will allocated funds for the Franklin Library Association, a library association in Medway, and a fund to benefit the library in Manchester, NH, where he had made his fortune as an industrialist.

As the Universalists completed a college, and added a parish school, the town moved to expand its own schools. In 1868, a high school was set up with a first class of 22 students. An 1879 map indicates that the high school was held along with a grammar (middle), and elementary school in the Red Brick School still located at the intersection of Main Street and Maple Street.

Meanwhile, an old friend of the association had determined to make his own contribution. In 1870, William Makepeace Thayer, at that point resident in Boston, wrote to his friends and colleagues.

To the officers & members of the "Franklin Library Association", in Franklin

Gentlemen,

It is with great diffidence that I address you on the subject of books as an addition to your library.

By an accumulation of books on my shelves from various sources; some by purchase, but mostly from families of relatives here in Boston, deceased; I did, more than six months ago, fill several boxes with them & had them put into an upper room, solely for the purpose of getting them out of our way; still leaving a large bookcase filled with books, besides many left in closets, & on shelves.

It is but a short time since the idea came into my mind, that I would like to give these books to your Association, if they should be thought worthy of a place on the shelves of your valuable & well selected library; the catalogue of which I have examined with great pleasure & satisfaction. Hence the diffidence I feel in offering these books; as I do not consider them any choice selection but rather a promiscuous collection of almost every kind, & on almost every subject. Some new volumes, but mostly such as have been used some in families, the bindings still being mostly pretty good. But notwithstanding this variety as mankind are not all alike; but variously constituted, it may happen that this variety might find readers since those who are seeking knowledge on different & various subjects.

We live in an age when people will not be content to remain inactive as to the improvement of their minds; especially when the means of knowledge are within their reach & of so easy attainment.

That Franklin people have always been a reading and intellectual people is a characteristic trait of them, well known for many years in the towns round about them. This reputation as a reading and intellectual people is undoubtedly attributable, in a good degree, to the means & opportunities they enjoyed (& improved) by having libraries, so early established, among them.

Dr. Emmons says in his "Sermon addressed to the congregation in Franklin, March 1st, 1787 upon the occasion of receiving from Dr. Franklin a donation of books", that there was a Parish library established here "in order to improve their minds in useful and divine knowledge" more than thirty years before that event. Dr. E. adds, "This library has been highly beneficial to the people of the parish"

As it is the duty of all to improve their minds in every branch of human knowledge & as we have been endowed by our maker with natural powers, capable of improvement, this lays us under obligation to improve our powers & faculties to the best advantage; not only for our own benefit; but, also, for the best good of others.

Knowledge & Learning are useful in every situation & station in life; he, therefore, who applies himself to the acquisition of knowledge is preparing himself for usefulness in the world & fulfilling the design of his [creator?]

I have already been a member of your Association, you will probably remember, in full communion with you, more than ten years; having been elected a Life Member by your kindness; and shall always be happy to know that the "Franklin Library Association" is in a flourishing condition.

And, that I feel quite an interest in the affairs of your town, may it seem strange, I trust, when it is remembered, that Franklin is my native place; that I've spent more than forty years of my early life, actively engaged in business.

There, too, in your churchyard, I shall remember while I live, that my honored and dearly loved parents & many dear relatives quietly rest, waiting Gabriel's Trumpet to wake them, & all of us to meet our Lord & Judge when time shall be no more.

The books I herewith send you are given with the hope that they may be the [?] in some small degree, of interesting the young people of Franklin in seeking after knowledge; such knowledge as will enable the possessor to be useful here, & happy hereafter.

18 Harvard St. *Wm Makepeace.*

Boston, March 2nd, 1870

P.S. I have put into Box no. 6 my photograph, though at the time I had some taken I had not thought of such a thing; nor do I suppose that you will feel any particular interest in having it, but, as it is a spare one with me, I have sent it, and shall be the one gratified at having it hung up in your library room as being next to coming among you myself.

W.M. ------

Presumably, the Association accepted the gift graciously.

Meanwhile, at the end of December, 1874, the Association had gathered Benjamin Franklin's books for examination before the annual report to the directors of the association. "The committee availed themselves of the opportunity just afforded to thoroughly re-arrange all the books, and place upon the shelves a large number of volumes that have been laid away for want of room." The original collection had been supplemented with 100 new books from the `Farmer's Library.'

The members of the Association were as eager to systematize and organize the library as they were to expand it. "We have also purchased nearly two hundred volumes of new and popular works, and thought it best to prepare a new catalogue which shall include all the books now in the library, and arrange them with more system than has been attempted before. The reading public, or that portion of it who have drawn books from the library the past season have no doubt found our list of books, as comprised in *two catalogues* and *four supplements*, very inconvenient to all concerned."

In February, Franklin's constable, William E. Nason, issued the warrant for the annual Town Meeting, which was held in early April. The *Franklin Register* wrote, "We do not propose to discuss these matters in our columns... They were very generally and generously ventilated at the town meeting; but we may be pardoned for saying that it would have been more creditable to the town if more harmony could have prevailed." In spite of a lack of harmony, under the guidance of moderator James M. Freeman, the residents were able to agree to grant $200 to the Association. Other items included restraining pigs and mules from roaming free and purchasing a "hose carriage" for the Fire Department.

At year's end, Franklin's rising star industrialist, James P. Ray, hinted at the public spiritedness that he would increasingly show for the library, by donating many barrels of flour to poor residents without fanfare. "We sometimes honestly think that wealth belongs more in the hands of men like Mr. Ray than in our own, for he uses it to God's glory and we might not," wrote the *Register*.

A reader wrote into the paper, thanking Ray, "for a one hundred ninety six pound nugget of the `staff of life,' which was rolled into my kitchen on the morning of the 25$^{th}$." The letter to the editor added, "The sun, they say is `always shining,' yes, but we don't feel its *Ray-s*."
It seemed the Ray brothers were always present when improvements to the town were being discussed. In early October, 1876, they gathered together as the Friends of the Water Works,

with other citizens and a representative of the Holly Water Works in from Boston. When the Benjamin Franklin Savings Bank held its annual meeting in July of the same year, James was one of several vice-presidents, while Joseph sat on the trustees.
Local entrepreneurs cited the Rays for references, as in the case of D.P. Baker, who sold real estate and fire insurance.

The Rays also encouraged engagement with the big political questions of the day. Local and national politics were often the source of plenty of pageantry in the late 1800s and as the Hayes-Wheeler presidential ticket face off against the Democratic Tilden-Hendricks ticket loomed in the 1876 election, the Franklin Republicans hosted Union General Swift as a speaker. In spite of fog and looming rain clouds, large crowds thronged around the Town Hall, greeted by the ebullient firefighters and the local band. After the Trowbridge quartet choir sang, Joseph Ray introduced the visiting general, who spoke about the current events of the day, such as Southern indebtedness and rebelliousness in the former Confederacy. Ray then accompanied him back to Boston.

Joseph Gordon Ray

As Franklin entered the prosperous 1880s, interest in reading was high and endeavors to create local libraries were afoot in neighboring towns. In Medway, the Dean library (not to be confused with the subsequent book collection of Dean Academy) counted on private subscriptions, along with a similar association in Norfolk. The Dean Library announced in February, 1883 that it was adding 70 new books to its collection and its association planned to add books on a rolling basis, rather than in a once a year purchase in January. At the same time in Franklin, the library directors reelected Waldo Daniels as librarian.

In March, 1884, Norfolk notables discussed improvements to the town's subscription library. The news came alongside an announcement posted in the *Sentinel*, the new Franklin newspaper launched in 1879, issued by Waldo Daniels calling on all borrowers to return their books by August 2, 1884 or risk a steep fine of 10 cents per book.

As library fever seemed to be sweeping the area, even con men got in on the game. The *Sentinel* reported on July 17, 1884, that a young man passing through Sheldonville in West Wrentham had claimed to be a representative of the Franklin Square Library Company of New York, selling one-dollar subscriptions. He even set up a library location at the house of Barton Bay. Luckily for the people of Sheldonville, the con man did at least distribute 50 books, although the company in New York put a note in the paper setting the record straight.
In January, 1885, one citizen writing in the newspaper vented their frustration at all the excitement about libraries. "Somebody ought to make an effort to get an appropriation for sidewalks at the March meeting even if we have to cut down the amount devoted to the public library. Our feet need the money as badly as our heads."

During the summer of 1886, it seemed the library was running on irregular hours. Daniels put a notice in the paper inviting patrons to return when the library reopened on the Wednesday evening of August, 25th. Patrons were eager to have the library reopened—almost as eager as they were to see rail service expanded on the line to Woonsocket—and some demanded the trustees spend more of their funds on books.

With Benjamin Franklin's books graduated from their old storage in Dr. Emmons' barn and growing interests in libraries nationwide, Franklin became a source of inspiration for other communities. In 1890, visitors from 13 different states, as well a large group from Millis came to tour the library and see the original books. On April 25, it was announced the library would move to a new room on Dean Avenue and would close for a time. Patrons were told to return their books by May 7th.

As libraries grew in popularity, so too did efforts to regulate the books they contained. One *Sentinel* editorial in 1891 described things in particularly Biblical terms. "Now that plague of frogs [from the Book of Exodus] is back...It is smiting this nation. It comes in the shape of corrupt literature. These frogs hop into the store, the shop, the office, the banking house, the factory—into the home, into the cellar, into the garret, on the drawing room table, on the shelf of the library."

The lurid description continued, "While the young woman is reading the forbidden novelette after retiring at night, reading by gaslight, one of these frogs leaps upon the page. There is a vast number of books and newspapers printed which ought never to see the light. They are filled with a pestilence that makes the land swelter with a moral panic." The editorial went on to suggest that such "frogs" were responsible for many people being sent to penitentiaries and insane asylums.

"The longest rail train that ever ran over the Erie or Hudson tracks was not long enough to carry nor large enough to carry the beastliness and putrefaction which have been gathered up in bad books...in the last twenty years."

Away from the vitriol about "cheap literature," the library announced a new catalog and a reorganization in September, 1892, as it added 400 new books. A list of new books at the library released in 1896 gives a sense of some of the things people were reading at the time. *The Adventures of Sherlock Holmes* and the *Legends of King Arthur* catered to all ages, while *College Girls*, *Five Little Peppers*, and *Boy of Officers of 1812* met the interests of younger readers. For the curious, there were non-fiction titles as well such as *Europe in Africa in the 19th Century*, *Electricity for Everybody*, *Psychology and Education* or *Socialism.*

Even as spring drew closer in March, 1899, the growing stock of books kept plenty of people coming into the libraries, as the *Sentinel* noted. "The days have lengthened perceptibly but neither evenings nor Sundays are as yet too short for any young person, or old person, to fail to profit by the stores of knowledge and the means of self-improvement thrown open to everyone at the public library."

At a time still before the dawn of motion pictures, Franklinites enjoyed live performances at the Morse Opera House and the town music hall. Often performances and vaudeville shows were done to raise money. The Irish fraternal organization, the Ancient Order of Hibernians, held a week of shows in February, 1900 to raise money for its own small library. Contest winners were awarded with fine glassware. One contest had patrons vote on the "handsomest baby." One, Harold Colgan won with 927 votes, beating out fellow infant, Hazel Foster.

Chapter 4: Realizing the Ray Memorial

The birth of the Association came at a vital moment; rescuing the original books from Benjamin Franklin from disuse and neglect and coalescing the efforts of all those interested in books, learning, and the future of the town. But that did not mean there was yet a library in anything like a permanent sense. Rather, the "original" books and a growing accumulation of donations and additions lived a peripatetic existence, with few if any accompanying services. In short, accessing the books remained difficult due to the lack of a dedicated facility, revenue stream, or staff.

To be sure, such things had been discussed, but the time was not yet ripe.

In the early 1890s, Franklin and much of the nation were gripped by a serious recession with effects akin to the more famous Great Depression of the 1930s. Although the fallout of the recession was surely felt, Franklin at the time was often more preoccupied with local baseball games played between opposing teams in places like Caryville—a village on the Bellingham line—and Dean Academy's team, church events, factory work and annual harvests at the town's many outlying farms.

Within the town government, the 1890s brought a spillover of concerns from the 1880s, often involving alcohol. In light of high levels of drinking and perhaps the economic malaise, many social reformers had grown interested in limiting alcohol consumption and sales and some even pushed for outright prohibition. In the meantime, the town set about creating a task force of special officers larger than the regular police force to catch liquor license violators.

While the town troubled itself with the question of alcohol and economic growth, the members of the Franklin Library Association had their own set of affairs to consider.

For a town that was still quite small, Franklin's circulation was outstanding—over 10,000 items each year—supported almost exclusively by the Association with only a nominal $700 contribution from the town. Rev. W.M. Thayer, himself a famous local preacher and advocate of alcohol prohibition, had contributed a large private collection of 114 books throughout the years, which boosted holdings in combination with a gift from the accounts of the late Oliver Dean, who set aside funding for the Association in his will. These were all things on the positive side of the ledger but they only served to further highlight the need for a permanent home for the library.

News from Boston heralded help, but only of the most modest sort for now. The Acts of 1890, included chapter 347, 'An Act to Promote the Establishment and Efficiency of Free Public Libraries,' established the Free Public Library Commission of Massachusetts, which promised to disburse funds in the future, albeit from a very limited budget[iii]. For the time being, the Association was, for all practical purposes, the library. William F. Ray, of the highly successful local Ray family and an active member in the Association, submitted the group's report for the year 1890. It brims with excitement about some other news of particular interest from Boston which no doubt made Franklinites more conscious of their special distinction. "One of the eminent Librarians of the State, in a public address in Boston, a few months since, referred to the Franklin Library as the *first* Public Library in the United States. In view of this fact, the fame of Benjamin Franklin, the original patron of our Library... the example furnished in the provision made for Public Libraries in other towns of the State, can we not reasonably hope that in the near future some son of our town, by birth or adoption, may gladly furnish for our Public Library a permanent building that will be an architectural adornment to our streets and a monument to the thoughtful generosity of the donor?"

William F. Ray's words were to prove prophetic as members of his family ultimately took on the task of creating just such an "architectural adornment" to hold the town's founding gift.[iv]

New England, as one of the most industrialized places in America in the 19th and early 20th century, spawned a number of wealthy families imbued with a strong desire to give back to their communities. Franklin was no different, thanks to the dynamism of the Ray family.

James P. Ray was born in South Mendon in 1820. Growing up he received only a smattering of formal education at schools in Bellingham, Uxbridge and at a manual labor school in Worcester. In spite of his sparse education, he was a bright young man and ended up teaching school in Northbridge by the age of 15. James set his sights on business when he turned 17, but 1837 was a bad year to launch a business. A financial panic gripped the nation and James lost almost all of his money. With his remaining possessions valued at only seven dollars, he started up business once again.

Known to friends, family and neighbors as "Jimmie," the young Ray entrepreneur picked up where his own father had left off. The elder Ray had lost heart in his business after a failed deal with a company in Providence and Jimmie effectively became head of the family at age 18, supervising his woolen business and acting as a father figure for the entire family.

Jimmie's younger brother, Joseph Gordon Ray, was also born in Mendon, 11 years after his older brother on October 4, 1831. By 1839, at the age of 8, he was already earning his "keep" at Jimmie's mill. Seven years later, he declared himself an independent agent and started the first rag picking business of its kind in New England. With most materials still scarce and manufacturing highly expensive, 19th century society put great emphasis on the reuse of materials that might today be thrown out. That meant reprocessing old textile scraps into a new material—known as shoddy. Joseph launched the largest shoddy operation in the region at just 15 years of age.

By 1851, the entrepreneurial brothers decided to merge their enterprises and it wasn't long before the established mill owners in the area began to take notice. Frank Ray, another brother, briefly joined the venture but backed out in 1860.

The partnership of the two brothers proved fortuitous. J.G., as Joseph came to be known, was highly adept at the mechanical workings of a textile mill but lacked Jimmie's shrewd financial sense. One journalist, after his death, wrote that J.G. would take "business gambles that would have put the owner of a Boston clipper ship to shame." In fact, J.G. was financially wiped out financially in 1844, perhaps prompting the partnership.

The brothers made it through the Civil War, but were hit by "Black Friday," a financial panic in 1873 that devastated New England businesses, particularly coming on the heels of the Great Boston Fire a year earlier. Miraculously, the Ray Mills survived unscathed. It was no miracle, just common sense. J.G. later revealed that he had stashed aside an emergency fund for such an eventuality. Even more importantly, the fund was held in gold, which would retain its value, rather than paper currency.

The Ray's also had a close escape in 1873, this time involving a skittish horse. As reported by the *Franklin Register*, on Friday, Aug. 1, "A horse belonging to Mr. F.B. Ray, attached to a buggy, while standing hitched in front of Mr. Butterworth's store last Wednesday afternoon, became frightened, and breaking away from his fastenings, started off on a wild race up the street. Another of Mr. Ray's buggies was standing near, in which was seated Mr. William Ray, son of Mr. F.B. Ray, and the frightened animal dashed his buggy against this one, oversetting it, but fortunately Mr. Ray was uninjured, though thrown violently to the ground. Near Capt. Spear's fish market, the horse broke loose from his buggy, by smashing the shafts, and then ran wildly up the street. Numbers of persons were near at the time of the disaster, but no one was hurt."

While the *Register* generally maintained a tone of respect if not awe toward the town's most prosperous citizens, it wasn't above delivering the occasional gibe. One issue remarked on "the grounds around the elegant residences of Jas. P. Ray and Joseph G. Ray are nearly graded, and they begin now to show how elegant they will be when fully completed and the fences are all put up." Then, winding up to a punch line, the author continued, "the sidewall will no doubt be constructed on a scale of similar liberality, thus forming an unbroken line of good work down to the corner of Mr. Fletcher's lot, which we hope to see in proper trim before long,-- the sidewalk there being sadly out of order, and quite out of keeping with the value of the property behind it."

The mid-1800s were a time of railroad mania, in which America was quickly gridded with brand new rail ventures—many of which failed. But the Rays were nonplussed and saw a need for a railroad in the area. Borrowing a page from the Van Sweringen brothers in Cleveland, the Rays took in business partners to finance a line. Financiers in Boston chuckled at what they must have thought were "crazy" hinterland businessmen from Franklin, working to build a line between

The Ray block on Main Street in Franklin was one of the many business interests of the Ray family.

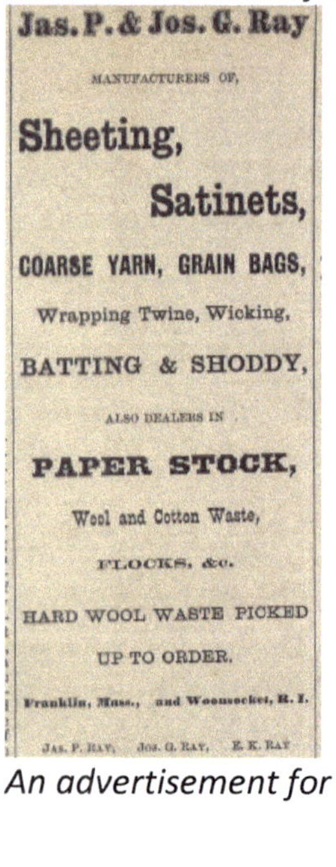

An advertisement for the Ray business from the Franklin Register, *1873*

Milford, Franklin and Providence. But they were proved wrong. The Rays managed to turn a handsome profit with the later sale of their rail line and the business helped ensure that Franklin businesses had ready and affordable access to supplies and markets.

With the money obtained from the project, the Rays built up the felting part of their textile business, which would later reap significant profits. Non-woven felt was widely in demand for hats and clothing. By the late 1880s, the Rays found themselves running 14 mills representing every part of the textile industry and were courted by bankers from Boston and New York City, with their money invested in top of the line securities. The Ray brothers were very active in different hobbies. Joseph Gordon, for instance, put his money toward improving the dairying industry in Massachusetts.

Throughout their lives, both brothers were members of the Universalist church—the antecedent of today's Franklin Unitarian-Universalist community—and donated extensively to the congregation. The Ray brothers were worldly men, but still valued a sense of place and belonging in Franklin. In fact, both brothers married locally. James married Susan Knapp, a Franklin resident, with whom he had two sons, Edgar and James F. Ray. His brother, meanwhile, married Emily Rockwood, from Bellingham and had two daughters. The two daughters, Lydia Paine Ray and Anne D. Ray, carried on the family tradition of living in Franklin and upheld the civic spirit of the family as adults. Lydia married Arthur Peirce while her sister married Adelbert Thayer.

In fact, Frank Ray, the other Ray brother who had briefly participated in the textile business, had five children, two sons, Williams and Charles, as well as three daughters, Mabel, Margie and Maude. However, none of his descendants took up the family torch. One brother, Charles, did end up becoming an independent business owner, but relocated to the Midwest.

As the brothers grew older, they grew tired of the attitudes of Boston and Providence bankers and built the Ray building on Main Street—one of the largest brick office buildings in western Norfolk County at the time—to house the First National Bank. Before the advent of steam fire engines, Joseph Gordon Ray dug deep into his own pockets to finance a hand-pump fire engine to protect Franklin against conflagrations.

The start of the 20th century left some Franklinites anxious about the future, especially with the death of some of the town's leading lights, such as Joseph and James Ray. At a temperance meeting at the Universalist church, Dr. Hodge lamented the changing community. "We are confronting new conditions in Franklin. We have these electric railways connecting us with neighboring towns, bringing as our tradesmen hope, increased trade to Franklin; affording, now that they say the bicycle is going out of fashion, opportunities for pleasure seeking; bringing toughs and idlers and drunken men into town, and making it easy for our own vicious ones to get to the saloons of liquor selling towns. The quiet and simplicity which were the claim of Franklin are gone and gone forever."

Dr. Hodge called for any local office holders favorable to liquor sales to be thrown out of office and pitched his own vision for the future of the town. I want to see this a beautiful town. Our town hall could very possibly be improved upon. I want to see handsome public library building; I want to see federation among the churches. I want to see increased intelligence."

However, for most people, the talk of the town, was the expansion of the street railway to Woonsocket. Others circulated a petition calling for a street railway directly to Medway.
Big changes were coming to the town in 1901, seemingly fulfilling some of Dr. Hodge's hopes. Construction of the Ray Memorial Library had begun along with the Ray science building at Dean Academy. As work on the two buildings proceeded through the winter, under the direction of "contractor McCarthy," the library stayed open in its regular quarters. Borrowers were reminded to return their books in July for an annual inspection, after which the library would open to the public on Saturday evenings in August.

When the new library building was first proposed, the design included a small building at the back to house the boiler. However, as the project went along the contractors decided to move the boiler into the basement in March, 1902. They had to smash through a section of the southeast corner to access the basement and added an outside concrete-covered coal pocket to fuel the boiler. They promised the new space in the basement would be well lit and fire proof. "This change will improve the rear of the building, and will afford a better opportunity for the landscape gardener's work." Warm weather in early March left the contractors eager to get back to work after the long winter, but a sudden snowstorm put the project on hold for a little bit longer.

By June, the granite facing of the library was nearly complete. "On every hand are heard the comments at to the elegance of the new structure. Construction is about completed to the windows, leaving but little more of the exterior than the sloping roof to be done. A course of brick inside gives the building added solidity...Visitors from out of town are greatly attracted by the building and universal commendation is heard." The item shared the page with news of the graduation of William F. Ray and Joseph Gordon Ray (son of Edgar K. Ray of Unionville) from Brown and Tufts respectively.

The reporter added that the adjoining Ware property had been added to the library property. Built 30 years earlier by Abijah Rockwood, it had nearly abutted the Fales grocery store on the first floor of the Daniels Block, which was the town's only amusement hall, on the second floor in the 1880s. To the rear had been skating rink and the Daniels straw hat factory. A devastating fire had swept the area on May 27, 1886, leaving only the small house and the nearby Grace Universalist Church standing.

On November 18, 1902, the library received a unique gift from Thomas Lawson, a Boston millionaire and sailor who had built the yacht *Independence*. "*The Lawson History of the America's Cup*, an elegant book published in the most superb style of the printer's and bookbinder's art. It is intended only as a star book to be perused at the library reading room...It is probably the most expensively gotten up book in the library."

At the same time, a fundraiser sold $16 worth of certificates to help finance the new library. A seventh-grade class under tutelage of Miss Flora Whiting sold 50 certificates in total.

A private exhibition highlighted the work of Tomasso Juglaris, the artist commissioned to paint the library reading room. "[It] demonstrated the excellence and extent of Juglaris' conception of his task, since which time two painted compositions for the large panels that are to have position in the hallway of the library have been received.

In October, local professional, Dr. J.C. Gallison, took a break from exhuming a body for an investigation. "Such is fame even if malodorous," the *Sentinel* commented. He met up with Juglaris and his cousin H.H. Gallison, shortly before Juglaris was set to sail for Italy to spend the winter. Dr. Gallison had met Juglaris at his home in Turin five years earlier, where he had been surprised at the mementos of Giuseppe Garibaldi—the revolutionary and statesmen who had united Italy 40 years earlier—including Garibaldi's clothes. Juglaris had married the widow of the surgeon who attended Garibaldi in his final hours. Earlier in the fall, in September, Dr. Gallison had visited his cousin in Annisquam in Gloucester to see the new frieze being prepared for the library. "He describes it as promising to be a handsome piece of work."

On the outside face of the building, a shaft was added to wire electrical lights on November 21.

Contractor McCarthy told the *Sentinel* that he hoped to get the building roofed before the start of winter, but noted that he had faced numerous delays getting building material.

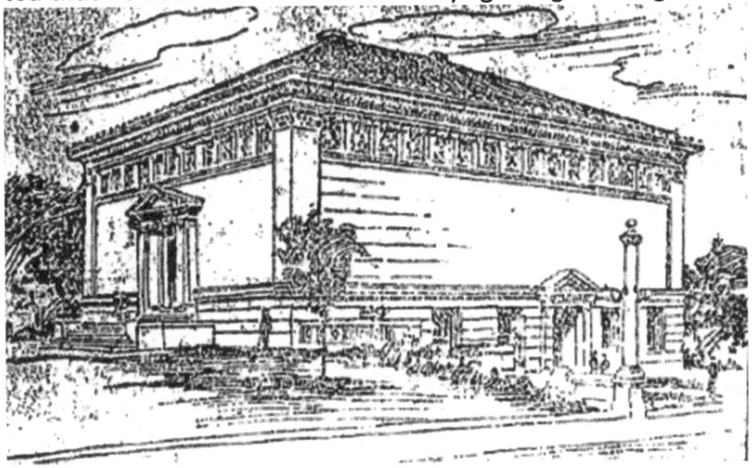

A new library in Belmont offered a very different feature than Franklin: A smoking room. In Belmont, "An invitation is extended to every resident of the town to smoke and read at the same time. As yet, however, the feminine contingent has elected other rooms in the building in which to pursue the current literature provided for them."

An amusing story emerged in August, 1903, when two plasterers—James Donahue and James Burke—were arrested for drunken and disorderly conduct and tossed in the 'hoosegow' in the basement of the Morse Block. Officer Redpath was on night watch duty, but while making his rounds, friends of the two plasterers broke them out of jail!

In June, 1903, the marriage of Lydia Paine Ray and Professor Arthur W. Peirce, at the Ray family's Elm Farm (current day Garelick Farms) was the talk of the town. One hundred fifty guests gathered, some from as far away as Philadelphia or Utah, and in spite of a rain squall mid-afternoon, the event served as a who's who of remaining notable Franklinites at the time. Portraits of Joseph G. Ray and his wife were on display and Adelbert Thayer served as the best man, while Charles and William Ray were the ushers.

By October, work was nearing completion on the library and the old Ware home was moved further back on the property. Meanwhile, the Woonsocket Electric Machine and Power Company was busily trying to convince the selectmen to give it a franchise to provide electricity for the town to expand lighting to small factories and businesses.

Finally, October 4, 1904, the great day arrived. "Nature put on her most smiling garb," noted the *Sentinel* in reference to ceremonies that began at 3 pm.

Former Massachusetts Governor John Davis Long (who served in office 1881-83), delivered one of the addresses at the dedication of the library:

"One of the most creditably distinctive features of Massachusetts is her public libraries. Of her 350 towns and cities not one is without that benefit. Nothing more eloquently than this fact could testify to her intellectual and moral culture. Hardly a hamlet within her borders that is not more than ancient Athens in the intelligence and cultivation of her people. Formerly, more than now, many of these libraries, the book more vital than its cabinet, the meat more than the shell, were lodged in meager quarter, sometimes in a single room of some dwelling house, thereby perhaps all the more significant of the eager and unquenchable thirst for knowledge which has always characterized the New England spirit. To-day the growing wealth and aesthetic taste of the time, often the loyalty of some grateful son or daughter of the town to his or her native or adopted heaty, has provided them the beautiful enclosures which adorn so many of our cities and villages with beautiful architectural effects.

"How fitting it is that this should be the case in this interesting and historic town of Franklin, which has a wealth of glory in its very name...."

"...While this building is unique in its purpose, it is yet – to the honor of our American civilization, be it said – only in the line and easy evolution of our New England system. It is as much a flower of the Pilgrim and Puritan seed, as much a part of the providential scheme of the Mayflower and of John Winthrop's landing, as much fused with the flavor of Harry Vane, as much a result of that vote of 1647, which declared that 'learning should not be buried in the graves of our forefathers,'

as is Harvard College or our common school system; of as if ever stone under its roof, every book on its shelves, every picture upon its walls, had been in the mind's eye of the founders of Massachusetts. Still more does it partake of the elements of our later consummations – our marvelous industrial growths. In its very amplitude, it yet embodies the idea of that homely saving economy, that intelligent thrift, that careful provision for future needs, which characterizes New England. It embodies the idea of those great agencies and massings of skilled and citizenized labor, which at once employ a multitude of hands and at the same time stimulate as many activities of invention and brain, and so combine manual toil and intellectual genius in that splendid union of which our national institutions are at once the cause and the result.

"In the engrossments of everyday life, few of us appreciate what a universal blessing a library is. I have been surprised and delighted in my observations of our towns, to find how generally people of all conditions of life and degrees of means depend upon the public library; of how many a sickroom its outflow is the light; of how many a poor man's home it is the cheer; of how much leisure and ennui it is the relief; and how thoroughly well informed and well read the community is made by its resources...

"The Ray Memorial Library! As you think of the scope of its noble and far-reaching beneficence, with what gratitude you turn to those who gave it, although I know they would prefer no public reference to their benefaction. It stands as a memorial to those who made the name it bears a synonym for personal worth and public spirit in this community and to whom the best tribute is in their own life work which is an open book before you, and in the cordial responsiveness with which you, their fellow-citizens, who knew them through and through, have gathered to honor them in dedicating it. It emphasizes the example of good and true lives, and so suggests not the least significant lesson of this hour. For what better inspiration can we have than to recall the honest industry and brave purpose of a career which, like that of Joseph Gordon Ray, in early youth overcomes all adverse circumstances; which conquers success; which lays out and walks a broad way of comprehensive and benevolent business enterprise; which puts a generous public spirit into every step and so commands general respect and confidence and the honors and duties of public trust, and which wins fortune to spend it again in helpful return to the sources from which it came."

Public reaction to the new building was immediate and enthusiastic, with stories appearing nationally.

An early interior view of the Ray Memorial Library.

The Craftsman, a periodical focused on the arts, provided a lengthy and adulatory write up (published in 1905) by Irene Sargent, an American art historian and leading advocate of the American Arts and Crafts movement.

"As a monument to civic art, the Ray Memorial Library, just completed in the manufacturing village of Franklin, Massachusetts, will lend great distinction to that community for a long period to come. Locally standing for something which the outsider can not fully realize, since it perpetuates the remembrance of a worthy, enlightened, public-spirited citizen, it possesses, beyond this sentimental quality, an aesthetic value which entitles it to national consideration."

"The Library stands "somewhat back from the village street," facing the famous old Dean Academy, a large red brick structure of non-descript architecture, adjacent to a church built of white stone, and of which the principal exterior feature is an English Gothic painted window. Into these surroundings the chaste severity of the Greek line and mass brings an element accordant with New England traditions. Set within sufficient free space to display its characteristics, the Library, like an ancient temple-prototypes, gives the impression of size by means of its perfect proportions, rather than by actual measurements. It is built of granite, like the stone of the Boston

Public Library; its façade gaining dignity by the unbroken wall which rises, devoid of windows, to a point just above a pediment of the slightly advanced Ionic portal. Then, monotony is prevented in the exterior, while, at the same time, the purpose of the building is suggested, and the interior provided with daylight in the most desirable manner by the system of fenestration which, carried completely around the building, is broken at short, regular intervals by pilasters rising from simple moldings: a device giving a rhythm and accent very pleasing to the eye. Above this, the plain band serving as a frieze, preserves the chasteness of the design and does not prevent the eye from rapidly seizing the plan, as would be done by sculptured ornament. This plain frieze, capped by a cornice of sharp profile, is thus contrasted with the latter member, and by this simple means the façade is again saved from insignificance; since that which may be termed the projecting brow of the building lends dignity to the structure, just as the prominent forehead and sometimes an overhanging throw of drapery were given, with the same intention, to the human face by the late Attic school of sculptors. In this well calculated exterior effect the portal is allowed due importance; constituting a type and model of its kind, while remaining chaste and restrained enough to comport with the prevailing style. In this feature, material and design concur in a whole to which the eye returns again and again, gratified by a harmony and refinement of proportion which are truly Greek. Nor is any detail omitted which could add to the completeness of the scheme, such as the bronze door, having as its sold ornament the egg-and-dart molding, the bosses of which are slightly tinged with vert-antique. Another detail of the exterior especially worthy of mention exists in the low screen-wall seen at the right of the illustration. This wall, divided into three descending sections, by the very fact of these divisions, offers variety to the eye as it directs as it directs it to the column supporting electric lights placed at the boundary of the library lot; thus unifying a street fixture with the building proper. The columns at first excites comment as presenting a composite capital, and being therefore at variance with the general scheme. But this detail is justified when the spectator pictures to himself the effect of an Ionic capital, which should replace the actual existing one; substituting for graceful plant-like forms the flat cushion with its large volutes, designed always to be placed beneath an entablature. Again, the screen-wall breaks the square outline of the building which, in the absence of this device, would be too aggressive in its isolated position. The wall further and principally serves to modulate the difference in level between the façade and the side of the building, which latter by this arrangement affords sufficient height to be pierced by a series of basement windows, and by a second doorway treated simply, in order not to detract from the chief entrance.

As a whole, this exterior, apparently so lacking in complexity, is found to be the result of the most careful, intelligent and skilled architectural work. It prepares the spectator for the beauties of the interior; in the same way that the overture attunes the ear and mind of the listener to the musical scheme which is to follow, by presenting the principal motifs in their unadorned force.

Through the beautiful Ionic portal previously described, the visitor enters a spacious vestibule known as the Memorial Hall. This occupies the entire width of the building; having a floor plan of twenty by sixty-two feet, and a height equivalent to two stories. Arrived here, one feels no diminution of flaw in the antique spirit announced by the exterior. Marble, bronze, mural paintings, and rich wood combine in a result recalling the descriptions of the classical authors when treating of civic structures. Here the strongest color-note is given by the red-brown of mahogany, which appears with a soft, dull surface. Red again occurs in the floor laid in brick , and this color is heightened by the dark green given to the walls, above the facing of black marble running like a wainscot about the hall, and itself topped by a band of Numidian marble, from which rise pilasters of the same stone, dividing the space into wide panels up to the bronze frames of the mural paintings, which form a frieze about three sides of the hall.

The color scheme here employed is one which might have easily become heavy and somber, but it is saved from such fault by the use in the ceiling of a bluish-green, which shows a find appreciation of the nature of color; since one element of the combination, the green, acts as an opiate, or anodyne, to the eye; while the other, blue, gives the effect of space and distance. This color, which is shaded, is acted upon by the daylight transmitted through the prismatic glass and thus acquires a luminous golden quality most valuable in the decorative scheme.

The Memorial Hall derives its name from the large, effective, bronze dedicatory panel set into the wall facing the entrance and bearing the inscription:

"In memory of Joseph Gordon Ray and Emily Rockwood Ray, this building is dedicated by their daughters, A.D. MCMIV. Quam dulce est minimisse.*"*

Spaces, already bounded by bronze frames, are also reserved for the portraits of the persons in whose memory the Library was erected, and at the left of the entrance, on the end wall, and over the black marble staircase descending to the Lecture Hall and the Children's Room, appears a landscape of Mr. Henry H. Gallison of whose qualities as an artist we shall have later ample occasion to speak. The subject of this picture, like the themes of the mural decorations here found, and in common with all similar work seen in recently erected American libraries, makes distant, rather than direct, allusion to books and the scholar's life. "The Dream City" is a fitting title for this canvas representing domes and minarets illuminated by a morning sun-burst, and set high upon a cliff which overhangs the sea, whose gray water stretch out to meet low-lying, leaden clouds.

As may be inferred, the Memorial Hall is, in all points, treated as a prelude to the rooms beyond. This is true especially of the frieze which, although strongly decorative, is here kept subordinate; while in the Reading Gallery the same feature becomes the most pronounced element of ornament. Both these schemes, the work of a single artist, although they are familiar as to their design, to all students of historic art, have yet a quality of extreme freshness; since our American school of mural decoration, following French traditions, has produced nothing susceptible of comparison with them. It is indeed interesting to study the design here employed; to select its various component elements – the antique, the Renascence, and the modern – and to note the skill with which they are combined. The subjects, also of very frequent occurrence, are interpreted so decoratively as to absorb and nullify all commonplaces. Line, mass and color so gratify the eye that the mind forgets to question the meaning of this or that figure, although conventions and symbols may be discovered in great numbers by those who seek allegories rather than pictures.

"Day" and "Night," the three divisions made of the twenty-four hours into periods of work, play and sleep – all these signify to one spectator a mosaic or bouquet of color, a structural scheme of lines, and equilibrium of masses, a study in chiaroscuro; while to another they may be simply beautiful illustrations of mythology in which it is a pleasurable task to identify each figure by its attributes; as for example: Prudence by her mirror; Vengeance by her dagger; and Fortune by her wheel.

In examining this frieze, no one acquainted with the history of art could attribute it to any but an Italian painter, so vividly does it recall the Vatican with its antique marbles, and the Roman palaces and villas with their frescoed walls and ceilings. Yet it is no painstaking copy of historic work, such as might be built from the notebook of a student. It simply shows on the part of the artist who produced it, a continuity of development from classical principles which has been preserved in him both by racial instinct and teaching.

Occupying the central space of the wall facing the entrance, "Eight Hours of Pleasure" are represented in Raphaelesque drawing, but with a rhythm derived from the close study of Greek bas-reliefs and vase-paintings. The continuous sweep of the arms, the alternation of the nearer with the more distant heads produce upon the eye and impression equivalent to that which is made upon the ear by a well-accented musical theme composed in common time. The vision is further gratified by the draperies, whose broadly treated masses form the base of the composition, and are painted in sapphire-blue, green, violet, rose and yellow; the figures in this picture, as well as in all other portion of the frieze, being projected against a gold background.

The colors mentioned and their ground naturally suggest an early Christian mosaic, although they have a tapestry-like softness; an effect due alike to the material upon which they are designed, and to the process employed in painting them. The former is a specially woven canvas; while the peculiar process, although well known in Europe, was here used by Mr. [Tomasso] *Juglaris for the first time in America. In order to secure the results desired, the pulverized mineral pigment is mixed into a preparation of cobalt, spirits of turpentine and beeswax, which have been boiled together. The completed mixture has the consistency of jelly, and is diluted by the artist according to his needs. It must be separately prepared for each color; it must be rapidly used, and being once applied, can not be modified without peril to the tapestry-like effect; since a thick coating will give a result not unlike an ordinary oil painting. But the process properly accomplished, assures a canvas which improves with age and constantly acquired depth and tone. One can therefore imagine what the exquisite quality of the Juglaris frieze will be, when time shall have dulled the gold and veiled the first brilliancy of the colors.*

Sargent then goes on to discuss specific elements of the painted scenes before moving on to discuss the other main features of the library...

"From the Memorial Hall doors with large glazed panels permit and uninterrupted view of the Delivery Room and the Reading Gallery. The latter, entered through the door at the right of the

dedicatory tablet, fills the office of the cella *in the antique temple, in that it is the place in which culminate the beauty and richness of the entire structure.*

"This large room is furnished in Spanish mahogany, showing pure Ionic lines and details; the volutes and dentils being works out with extreme delicacy. The dominant note of red is continued in the floor, which is of smalto, *similar to that used in Italian houses; a concrete of cement with small shells, or stones, piercing the reddish brown body with minute points of white. The movable furnishings of the room – the seats, chairs and tables --- are of the same mahogany as the finish and follow the same delicacy and suavity of line. The chairs especially, as they are symmetrically grouped about the tables, please by their refined,*
graceful profile, and cause surprise in the mind of the visitor that this pure model occurring in vase-paintings and other Grecian antiquities, has not been previously accepted by cabinet-makers to the exclusion of the grosser Empire type. The classic effect of the room is further heightened by a rich bronze cornice molding, displaying the scroll-and-honeysuckle pattern, by a bas-relief set in the chimney-piece, and by lamps, all of the same metal. Other artificial light is provided by a closely-set row of electric globes, defining an oval described within the quadrilateral figure formed by the ceiling, which is tinted very slightly green.

These materials and colors so judiciously employed, compose an admirable background for the second and much more important series of mural pictures painted by Mr. Juglaris. In this instance, they form a continuous decoration like a frieze, but rise from a level five and one-half feet above the floor-line to a height of twelve feet. They are painted upon a single piece of canvas, two hundred and forty feet in length, and are framed by a border composed of a double Greek key painted in soft yellow upon a light green background; adding a height of four feet to the decoration.

"The city, as the parent of culture, and therefore to be recognized by one of the most prolific of modern means of diffusing knowledge – the library – is accordingly represented at the beginning of the continuous picture; the sharp flanks of an acropolis, with the temples enveloped in an azure haze, being displayed upon that portion of the canvas which is fitted about and above the doorway leading to the Delivery Room.

"Considered as a whole, the decoration represents the course and the incidents of the festival; the processions of those who honor the god—ordered according to the various functions of the participants—issuing from the city-gates, advancing along the terraces and through sacred groves of the temple; then, upon the opposite wall, its arrival before the high-priest, while the altar-fires are alight and the sacrificial lamb lies bound ready for offering...."

..."Showing no traits of the copyist, Mr. Juglaris belongs to the comparatively small number of his compatriots who have really assimilated the principles of classical art, and have used them to their own delight, in the spirit of Michaelangelo, when in his blind old age, he was led daily to the colossal torso of Hercules, that he might follow with his hands the lines of its superb muscular development.

"The festival procession, therefore, constitutes an excellent school for the study of the human figure, as rendered by the Greeks, draped or semi-nude, and students of the fine arts throughout the United States would make a wise expenditure of time and means by visiting the Library at Franklin, with a purpose similar to that which prompts students of music to make much personal sacrifice that they may hear Wagner operas at Bayreuth.

And, finally, Sargent address the features of the Delivery Room.

"One other decorative feature of the Library is worthy of extended consideration, but it can receive justice only from the visitor; since words fail to render its peculiar quality, and mechanical means of reproduction are equally inadequate to the task. This is the frieze of the Delivery Room, painted by Mr. Henry H. Gallison, to whom the first artistic idea of the building itself is also due. The four paintings composing this decoration, alike in subject and treatment, defy any but the most summary description. They represent the great deserts of the world, viewed under various conditions of time of day and atmosphere: moonlight, twilight, mid-day, and sunset. In one instance, a silvery tone permeates the picture, transparent yet strangely dominant; in another, the silhouettes of mosques and minarets are projected against the sky, which is felt to be rapidly turning from the bronze of the late sunset to the cold, gray steel effect of nightfall. In a third, responsive to the direct rays of the sun, steaming vapor rises from the wide stretch of sand, which extends to meet the sky, giving the effect of an evil force of Nature, hostile to life, and showing no mark of man's passage, except in the ruined and half-buried temple which appears in the foreground. A fourth offers a less depressing scene: an oasis and pool in the distance, tinged with brilliant evening red; the only sinister suggestion lying in the birds of prey and carcass, which are painted in the contrasting waste of sand of the foreground.

"The beauty of these pictures, in common with all other examples of Mr. Gallison's work resides in the exquisite adjustment of values; a considerable distance being necessary to their proper effect, and this given, they fall into their places, like the notes of the musical scale. It is greatly to be regretted that these transcripts of the desert are obscured in the subdued light of the Delivery Room, and thus lose much of the force and charm which give to their author a distinctive place

among American landscape painters. But still their presence is felt, and the breadth of treatment apparently increases the dimensions of the small room which they decorate.

In the wake of the construction of the new library, the Ray Memorial Association was established with funding from the Ray family to see to the maintenance of the structure. Working in parallel, the two associations faced the decades ahead with confidence and a strong sense of a shared mission.

Before long, the novelty of the stunning new Ray Memorial Library building began to wear off and the structure became a part of the community. Adapting to demand and the realities of pre-air-conditioning life, the library was closed for the dog days of summer in August, 1905 except on Saturdays.

Even bigger than the 1904 celebration that accompanied the opening of the Ray Memorial Library, and no doubt partly inspired by the honor shown to his books in the creation of the new edifice, was the 1906 Benjamin Franklin Bicentenary, honoring the birthday of the town's benefactor and namesake. In addition to copious quantities of speechifying, exhibitions, and parades, the event was deemed so important that most employers gave their workers the day off! The *Sentinel* noted, "during the afternoon most of the blocks being finely decorated, among them being the Fletcher building, Hotel Windsor, the Ray building, Green's market, the Dana block, Metcalf's block, Reed & Searl's shop, Peck's store, Cataldo's building, Richardson's market, Farrington's store, Morse's block, Opera House block, and Mr. Singleton's residence."

Lieutenant governor Eben S. Draper of Hopedale spoke, noting, "I have always considered Franklin one of the greatest figures in American history" but reminded the listeners that the momentous times in which he lived were no less momentous than the present day with its promises and uncertainties. Former governor John L. Bates also spoke about Franklin and asserted both his Boston birth and the character evidenced throughout his life made him, in fact, a "Yankee."

One of the younger Rays, Maude Louise, also got into the act, reciting a poem of her own composition.

The creation of the new library provided new opportunities for children above all, many from families that might not have been able to afford books. The *Sentinel* reported in February, 1907 that throughout 1906 over 12,800 were taken out by children—one-third books for classwork and two-thirds fiction. "Few people have a sense of the remarkable hold which the Children's department...has upon our young people. No library within our knowledge begins to have so thoroughly equipped a children's department both as to management, arrangement and number of books."

Joseph G. Ray, the Ladies Social Circle of the Universalist Society, and others put together a big pageant in November, 1907, with singing, booths showcasing embroidery and an exotic array of cultures recreated in the library, such as a Japanese tea room and presentations about France, England and the Cherokees.

At the winter meeting of the FLA, Ella Campbell was re-selected as the librarian.

Local organizations frequently took advantage of the library to host community events. In April, 1908, the Baptist church gathered visitors from the Boston West Baptist Bible school. After lunch and a tour of the library, Reverend O.P. Gifford from Brookline spoke about keeping boys out of juvenile delinquency.

Henry Gallison brought guests from Europe, including a prominent Vienna medical family and Dr. Paul Clemen from Bonn, Germany, for a two-hour tour of the library.

Two blind students and their teacher from the Perkins Institute for the Blind did readings from braille of "Paul Revere's Ride" and "Alice in Wonderland," and showed off their knitting, sewing and crocheting in April, 1908. "The audience composed mostly of pupils of the sixth grade was intensely interested and lost not a word of the reading which was most expressive...Afterwards they escorted the two blind girls through the building, explaining the contents of the different rooms, and finally went with them to the station sorry to be obliged to part from them."

In some cases, photographs subbed in for guest speakers, as in 1908 when the Women's Education Association loaned a collection entitled "Gardens of Italy."

Guest speakers flocked to Franklin from more distant communities. Take for instance Elizabeth Merriam of South Framingham was a particularly engaging speaker. At a time when few people had the opportunity to travel overseas, she packed the lecture hall with eighth and ninth graders in February, 1909, telling of her trip from St. Petersburg to Paris. "Miss Merriam easily maintained her reputation as a delightful speaker."

Then there was Grace Lockhart, a storyteller from Boston with a "cultivated soprano voice," who entertained youngsters with songs and stories. Another story teller, Ethel Wood of Brookline, kept up more regular appearances for early elementary school students. On April 25, 1911, she made an appearance as an unofficial prelude to the May Festival for all ages being planned at the Morse Opera House.

Public health was on the minds of many in the 1910s, including the always forward-thinking Alden Club. In July, 1910, the organization arranged for the Health Library of the State Federation to visit Franklin for three weeks, making 40 books and pamphlets available for borrowers. "This library has been established for the purpose of encouraging persons to regain the health they may have lost," E.G. Campbell, the librarian told the *Sentinel*. In addition to written material, the traveling collection included 35 photographs of the state sanatorium in Rutland and others such as Sharon and Adirondack Cottage.

At the end of March, 1912, the Alden Club invited its sister clubs in surrounding towns to discuss conservation in the lecture hall at the library, with speakers like Fred Tucker, head of the state conservation committee and Mrs. Crocker, the chair of the Massachusetts State Federation of Women's Clubs. Crocker told the assembled women about the importance of children's gardens, soils and forestry, while Tucker laid out an overview of the topic and explained that "if our natural resources are not conserved that in a few hundred years posterity will suffer."

Only a few days later on April 12, as the *Sentinel* reflected on the event, a different kind of conservation was taking place at the library. The son of the editor of the *Franklin Register*, the town's first newspaper published in the 1870s donated bound volumes for the year 1873 and '74. R.R. Capron, the first editor of the *Sentinel*, who by then had moved to Western Massachusetts to become editor of the *Ware River News* sent over early editions of the *Sentinel* as well.

One guest speaker had led a civics class for grammar school students, but his attendees were disappointed when he had to cancel the class in 1915. However, Franklin remained a bit sleepy at times, far removed from the deadly events of World War I. By 1914, Ellen Hurd was serving as the librarian and in a reflection of a slow news day on August 4, as Europe was marching toward war, the newspaper reported that she was vacationing in Nantucket.

During America's participation in the Great War (World War I) the library took on some new roles. For instance, the *Sentinel* reported in March, 1918, on a big nationwide book drive.

"A Book Drive is to be conducted during the week of March 18, and every person is invited to contribute books from his private collection to be sent to our soldiers and sailors. Books taken to the Public Library marked "Library War Service" will be welcomed."

But patriotic sentiments did not extend to the local library for some patrons. The following month, the *Sentinel* was reporting that "certain people who use our Public Library mutilate the books, magazines and papers by tearing out pictures and items and writing in them.... The author went on to cite state law that prescribes a find of not less than five and not more than fifty dollars or imprisonment for up to six months for those charged and convicted of such actions.

Nor was national economic prosperity during the "Roaring 20s" enough to dissuade robbers from targeting the library. The *Sentinel* reported a break-in in early December, 1923, the fourth in recent years. The thieves had taken $7 collected for fines and littered the floor with matches, which they had used to see their way around.

Arthur W. Peirce served as both the headmaster of Dean Academy and president of the Franklin Library Association throughout the 1920s. At the annual meeting in January, 1924, other officers included Judge Orestes T. Doe, vice-president, Alice Wiggin, clerk, George Wiggin, Lydia Ray Peirce, Annie Ray Thayer, Arthur W. Hale and Dr. R. K. Marvin, directors. At the time, the Association had two sub-committees. Peirce, Doe and Thayer were on the executive committee, while Peirce, Wiggin, George and Alice Wiggin and A.R. Ray served on the book committee. They voted to keep Ella G. Campbell as librarian.

Other organizations also used the library for meetings. The Franklin Nursing Association held its annual meetings in February, electing officers and reviewing their finances. At a home before large scale health insurance, the organization counted $2659 in donations, $892 from fees and $725 from Metropolitan Life at its February, 1925 meeting.

Franklin marked its sesquicentennial—the 150th anniversary of the town's incorporation—in 1928. The festival centered on the downtown and drew thousands into the library to view a collection of books and mementos that once belonged to Benjamin Franklin and Dr. Emmons.

The Ray Memorial Library—the current home of the Franklin Public Library—is shown in this postcard from the 1910s, a few short years after its construction in 1904. The building was the result of philanthropy and public spiritedness on the part of the Ray family, which launched many of the town's mills and built the dairy farm later to become the Garelick dairy processing plant.

Chapter 5: Times of Turmoil

The beginning of the 1930s brought with it the crushing blow of the Great Depression, following on the heels of the 1929 stock market crash. In Franklin, the Depression was felt hard with many laid off, or put on reduced hours. It proved to be a difficult time for the town, followed closely thereafter by the global struggle of World War II. Fortunately, Franklin proved resilient throughout.

At the Ray Memorial, the library may have begun to attract fresh attention to concerns of jobless and disaffected. Sadly, library and Library Association records throughout these early and middle decades of the 20th century often prove sparse. At a time when budgets were tight and Franklinites desperate for growth and change, the town often omitted reports from its annual town report, or simply published a large itemized list of expenditures broken down by categories—a massive publicly available accounting sheet so that residents could understand where their tax dollars were being spent.

Because the Ray Memorial was managed primarily by a private non-profit, many years passed in which the report of the Library Association was simply omitted. Thankfully, years such as 1930, 1932 and 1937 featured more detailed reports that help us to understand the history of the Association throughout this troubled time in Franklin's past.

In 1930, the Ray Memorial was open on weekdays between 2:00 and 5:30 p.m. Librarians were then given a break for supper, and returned to reopen the library for another two hours between seven and nine at night. Instead of closing during July and August as it once had, the library remained open, but with reduced hours, opening at three in the afternoon. As Alice Wiggin put it, writing for the Board of Directors, "This change was appreciated by the regular patrons of the library."

Sure enough, as an early sign of the Depression, borrowers increased by 136 people, although Franklin's entire borrowing population hovered just around 1453. For the entire year, circulation reached 17,281, a substantial increase from 1929. Aiding the library in purchasing 200 new books, borrowers who had lost or returned books late paid over $75 in fines. Witnessing rising demand from the public for more books, the Association requested an additional $2000 for 1931.

The existence of the Association was good news for borrowers. Even as town funds tightened, the Association could tap into its substantial, well-managed finances or source books through donation from other allied organizations in the community, such as the Alden Club, the Knights of Columbus and others. The Knights of Columbus, pursuing their role as the voice of the town's Catholic community, contributed the *Columbia Catholic* magazine to the Reading Room. The

Society for the Prevention of Cruelty to Animals chipped in *Our Dumb Animals*. At the same time, other shelves were occupied by titles such as the *Franklin Sentinel* or *American Poultryman*, in a nod to the town's innumerable truck farmers and poultry producers, serving the tastes and needs of nearby Boston.

Perhaps the greatest success story at the start of the decade was the Children's Department. Entirely privately funded, the department accounted for an enormous circulation and a large number of borrowers. Two-hundred fifteen borrowers were added in 1930, helping to boost circulation to 12,367.[v]

By 1933—the worst year of the Great Depression—the Library Association's reports had been whittled down in length and cut straight to the numbers. Circulation had risen, but only slightly, while book acquisition had nearly halved. Fortunately for borrowers, 23 books still came in during the year as gifts, but with only 136 items purchased, new material was a bit sparse. Being mindful of town finances, the Association requested a more modest $1500 for 1934 and thanked private donors "in kind" such as Mabel Wolff, Emma North and George Mason, along with public donors like the state and federal government. Over in the children's room, circulation was down by nearly a thousand items, perhaps as children shouldered the burden of jobs, work around the house and local farms (current child labor laws were not fully instituted until 1938).[vi]

As the Depression wore on, conditions improved for a few years in 1935 and '36, in many places, only to witness another dip or decline the following year in 1938. After a brief silence, spanning a few years, the Association resumed its reporting, making note of the death of library benefactor and Ray Memorial planner Lydia Ray Peirce, daughter of Joseph Gordon Ray, on December 18, 1936.

A few years earlier, a Boston reporter traveled to Franklin to visit the elderly Lydia. "You know, we, the Rays, are back numbers now," she said modestly. "But we, my sister, Mrs. Thayer, and myself, are still interested in Franklin and everything that concerns its welfare. As to the Ray Memorial Library and other tributes to the memory of my father and mother I would rather not say anything," she closed.

Although Lydia Peirce remained humble with the press, perhaps no words needed to be said. The monumental Ray Memorial Library spoke for itself—a lasting tribute to Franklin and her family that would survive long after her own death.

At the annual meeting in January, 1937, the Association voted on resolutions related to Peirce's death. They began by crediting and thanking her for her years of outstanding service and unmatched financial contributions to the library. "The Association hereby expresses its thanks and appreciation not only for the free use of the Ray Memorial Building, without any expense for maintenance, heating, lighting or otherwise, but also for the innumerable gifts and beneficences bestowed on the Library by Mrs. Peirce and her sister, Mrs. Thayer." The Association resolved to publish its gratitude in the local press. At the time, Mrs. (Annie Ray)

Thayer was elderly and bed-ridden and unable to attend the Association's proceedings.[vii]

As the difficult decade drew to a close, in 1939, the Association was able to report a total of 302 open days each year—no small feat at a time before air conditioning and with finicky winter-time heating.

As the secretary put it, "The Franklin Library is beginning to take the place which a public library should hold in a town, i.e., guide to information or source material; opportunity and inspiration for use of leisure time in reading; chance for keeping up with periodicals not otherwise available to those of low incomes; and the starting of children [in reading]."

In these years, too, the Franklin Library Association appears to have been the recipient of largesse from an early supporter, Albert D. Nason. A Civil War veteran from Franklin, who relocated to Springfield in the 1880s with his wife Annie and their children, Mabel and Albert, Jr., where he became prosperous as the president of the Bay State Corset Company. There, he built a large home in 1888 in the fashionable new McKnight neighborhood. Albert died in 1903, and Annie died in 1934, outliving three of her children. Presumably after that date, a substantial bequest, totaling several thousand dollars, came to the Franklin Library Association, summarized in an undated, hand-written document apparently from the early 1940s.

In addition to traditional services like schools and public works, throughout the 1930s and 1940s, the library shared the stage with emerging government services created as a result of the Depression. Among these new services was the Work Projects Administration, better known as the WPA, which filed its own annual report describing its efforts to reemploy local laborers, often doing public service and improving infrastructure. In Franklin, the WPA could often be found building sidewalks or developing the new town pool on Beaver Brook, which is today the location of the Franklin Sculpture Park.

As the 1940s got underway, the US geared up for a war that it was not interested in fighting, although Americans were increasingly aware that conflict was brewing. As Franklinites dealt with the Valentine's Day blizzard of 1940 or the shocking news of the attack on Pearl Harbor, the Library Association's activities went on, though reporting on them seemed to have taken a hiatus "for the duration." For several years, the annual town report was pared down and the Association's report was omitted, perhaps as an effort to save paper during the war years. In fact, many original copies of town reports issued in the early and middle 1940s are made of the cheap, brownish-yellow paper, churned out quickly from cheap pulp as a result of the war.

The Association did issue its report for 1943 but kept it quite short, mentioning only the library hours and its officers. At the time, A.C. Ewen was the serving president, aided by vice-president Prince Crowell, treasurer A.W. Hale and secretary Alice Wiggin.[viii]

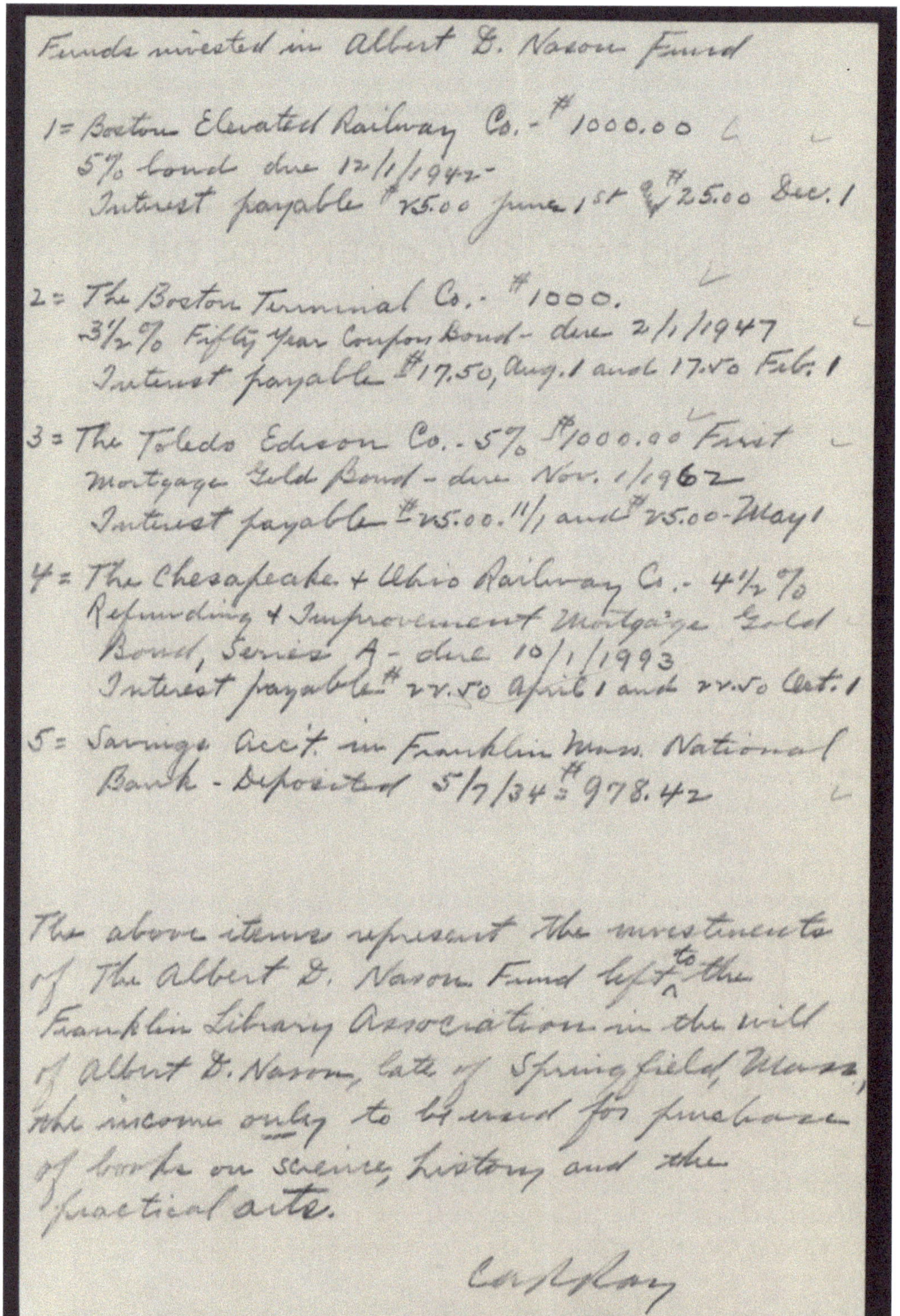

Funds invested in Albert D. Nason Fund

1 = Boston Elevated Railway Co. - $1000.00
5% bond due 12/1/1942
Interest payable $25.00 June 1st & $25.00 Dec. 1

2 = The Boston Terminal Co. - $1000.
3½% Fifty year Coupon Bond - due 2/1/1947
Interest payable $17.50, Aug. 1 and 17.50 Feb. 1

3 = The Toledo Edison Co. - 5% $1000.00 First
Mortgage Gold Bond - due Nov. 1/1962
Interest payable $25.00. 11/1 and $25.00 - May 1

4 = The Chesapeake + Ohio Railway Co. - 4½%
Refunding + Improvement Mortgage Gold
Bond, Series A - due 10/1/1993
Interest payable $22.50 April 1 and 22.50 Oct. 1

5 = Savings Acc't. in Franklin Mass. National
Bank - Deposited 5/7/34 = $978.42

The above items represent the investments
of The Albert D. Nason Fund left to the
Franklin Library Association in the will
of Albert D. Nason, late of Springfield, Mass.,
the income only to be used for purchase
of books on science, history and the
practical arts.

Carl Ray

Above, a summary of bequests from the estate of Albert D. Nason.

With the arrival of 1945 and the end to World War II, the Library Association prepared to adjust itself for more peaceful—and perhaps more prosperous times. The lineup of officers remained similar to what it had been in 1943, although Howard Lincoln now stood in as vice-president. The officers had expanded, with the addition of Kenneth Doe as auditor for the group's finances. Thankfully, with war's end, the town was apparently able to afford to print more ample reports. Following on circulation numbers from the early '30s, 1945 showed healthy growth with 29,000 items coming and going from the library.

Unlike the cash-strapped years of the Depression, 1945 also saw the addition of an astounding 755 books. Cheap, wartime paperbacks in the frontlines and at home had popularized leisure reading of everything from "serious" literature, non-fiction, and self-help books to crime and detective novels. Franklinites were apparently happy to participate in the trend. Unfortunately, it seemed that 1945 would be a bit of a slow year for the children's room, with only 5,046 items circulated.

The number of donors grew from previous reports, with a small list of private donors like Ethel Parker and P.S. Crowell and a growing number of periodicals available such as the *Christian Science Monitor*, *Woman's Home Companion, Polish Review* and *Netherlands Digest.*

Concerned about the aftermath of nearly 15 years of tight finances, the Association sought extra support from the town. Alice Wiggin closed her report with an appeal: "Again the Association must pay all bills in connection with the Library, including necessary repairs, postponed during the war years. In consequence of increased expenditures, the Association respectfully asks for the sum of five thousand dollars ($5000.00) plus the dog tax in order to keep the Franklin Library at its present level of efficiency.".[ix]

A year after the war's close, circulation fell by nearly a thousand items but remained at a healthy level. New purchases fell slightly as well but remained high above 1930s levels and included many unique and unusual publications. Among them was one periodical titled *Soviet Russia Today*. Although the Cold War would begin soon thereafter, the US and the Soviet Union were still on good terms after their mutual victory the year before and some people in Franklin were likely wondering what our old allies were up to.

Within the ranks of Association officers, Helen Feeley took over Alice Wiggins' role as secretary and Howard Lincoln moved into the role of president. Feeley submitted another request to the town for a $5000 sum to support the Association. The good news seemed to be that the town had in fact approved the prior year's request for funds and supplemented it, giving the library over $1,000 in addition to the $353 it had collected from fines. Nevertheless, with over $1,000 spent on new items and almost $2,000 dollars allotted for librarian salaries, the Association needed additional support.[x]

The following year, Helen Feeley once again prepared her report, joined among the officers by Ray Parmenter as vice-president and a new treasurer, John R. Goodwin. Juvenile circulation was up but for a second year, adult circulation was down—this time by an additional thousand items. Perhaps the explanation lay in Franklin's booming economy and thriving households, as adults returned from the war busied themselves with work and the newfound task of raising young families.

Expenses were higher than expected for 1947, as the library paid over $2,000 in salaries to the janitors and children's librarians as well as nearly identical sums as in 1946 for adult librarians and new books. Town funds materialized along the same lines as the previous year, but did not go as far to supporting overdue repairs and utilities, which found the library paying sums to the town water department and Worcester Suburban Electric Co. In other cases, different expenses turned up. A.J. Bullukian and Sons coal company charged $827 for deliveries during the chill winter and another $10 was spent "carting ashes." All the year's expenses left the library with a slight deficit of $29.

Nonetheless, 1947 was another success for the library. The only news of note was that donations of *Soviet Russia Today*, a periodical closely affiliated with communist groups in America, had ceased (the magazine stopped publishing a few years later, in 1951)![xi]

The late 1940s found Franklin speeding up its pace of change and growth as new industries, new houses and new families cropped up across the town. The Library Association was heartened to discover no deficit in 1949, thanks in part to additional funds from the town, more money from fines, and an ample $430 from the careful investments made by the Association.

Following on plans announced in 1945 for a town technical high school, which never materialized, the library launched Practical Arts classes to teach life and career skills to adults, sponsored by the School Department. All told, 60 men and women joined the program meeting in the Lecture Room, painting trays and furniture as well as hooking and braiding rugs. Helen Feeley described the classes with excitement, "These classes have brought new life and interest in the library building plus new borrowers for books."

After a slump lasting a few years, circulation finally recovered. Demand from new borrowers began to further boost circulation so the Association sought extra funds from the town in their 1950 report. Helen Feeley, writing for Ray Parmenter, the new president and new vice-president Rev. Trueman Menadue, summarized the Association's outlook heading into the 1950s. "With an ever-growing circulation, which this year increased almost 6000, it means that more people are using the library than ever before and that a large enough sum should be granted to keep it efficient."[xii] Efficiency and expansion weren't just buzz words—they were the reality of the year and a hint at the decade to come.

Chapter 6: The 1950s and 1960s

The 1950s—a glorious decade for the town of Franklin—dawned with many of the same key people involved in the Association, carrying on work begun in the '40s. Almost immediately, new concerns arose at the library, this time involving rowdy youngsters rather than tight finances.

Helen Feeley wrote an impassioned plea on behalf of the Ray Memorial: "The Ray Memorial Association, which owns the library building as well as its fine furnishings, has always assumed the responsibility of their maintenance. For nearly 40 years, they also paid for heat, janitor service and for the children's librarian. Franklin citizens have never paid rent for the use of this beautiful building. A glance at the large mahogany tables in the reading room which have been badly mutilated with names and initials of thoughtless boys and girls show how little some people appreciate the use of this fine room. In May, 1950, the R.M.A. had one of the tables refinished at considerable expense; less than two weeks later it had been cut and dug with various initials. It has now become necessary to have police protection at the expense of the town, for both the Ray Memorial Association and the Franklin Library Association feel that the library must be used for reading, studying or borrowing—not for gang meetings and rowdyism."

Fortunately, for all of their supposed "rowdyism" Franklin's youths were also boosting circulation, which had surpassed 8,000 for the children's department.[xiii]

By 1951, the trouble with the tables seemed to have righted itself. Instead of troublesome youngsters, the year's focus became more significant repairs. In place of mahogany tables, a leaky roof drew attention. Spearheaded by George Dana, William Garner, Richard Stack, Barnard Bachner, and Dr. James Howard, the Ray Memorial Association paid for costly repairs, although the organization's tight funds pushed interior renovations to water-damaged walls until a later year. According to Helen Feeley, "The Lecture Room, which is now used so much, is in great need of redecorating."

Although the Library Association remained concerned about lasting repairs, it had much to be happy about. Circulation remained steady close to 1949 levels, and even rose slightly. Donations of the *Christian Science Monitor, Catholic Digest, Rosicrucian* and *Living Tissue* helped to populate the shelves in the periodicals section, but one Frederick Carpenter received the bulk of the credit for annual donations. Carpenter donated a collection, "consisting of nearly 500 mystery, adventure and travel books."

As for the children and the children's section, the Association was grateful to the Aldenettes volunteer group (the women's auxiliary of the local Alden Club volunteer group) for running story hours and contributing "magiscopes and new books." To deal with the problem of rowdiness, the library brought on custodian Ernest Ward. "Since the advent of Mr. Ernest Ward, not only as a custodian of the library building, but as special police officer in the evenings, order and quiet are maintained in the reading room and in the stacks."[xiv]

Ever growing expenses found the Association looking into additional funds appropriated from the town and from traditional sources like the dog tax. The library's funding request for 1952 came to $8,500, only slightly more than the expenses for the town's Veteran's Department. Rising costs reflected both growing demand and changing value of money due to inflation.

The year brought with it one of the largest funding requests in the library's history up until that time, but also growth that made it seem like 1945 all over again. Once more, the library added nearly 1,000 items and close to 600 borrowers, and at last topped 30,000 items circulated. The Aldenettes and the Association introduced a plan to target young students in 1st through 4th grade for specialized book distributions, and quite literally rolled out a Book Mobile, set up by the Library Association. The Association rejoiced, discovering that circulation had grown by 2,568 items over 1951 totals.

The Aldenettes Community Service Department thought up other ways to meet the needs of children, sponsoring a Hobby Show in the springtime. Although the exact details of the Hobby Show were not written down, one can almost imagine children displaying paintings, doll and stamp collections, or the innumerable plastic ship and plane models appearing in stores in the 1950s.

The big news of the year, aside from rising circulation, was the completion of building repairs. "With the completion of the repairs on the library roof, making the building watertight once more, the Ray Memorial Association which assumes all repair bills, had the lecture room and the corridors downstairs redecorated with new lighting in the halls. These now present a fresh and bright appearance to the many users of the building." Undoubtedly, Helen Feeley was excited to see the redecorations that she had called for a few years earlier finally put in place.

Throughout the year, many of the same donors placed items in the library; E.W. Corr submitted *Catholic Digest*; and a number of new donations poured in from the Franklin Grange—a powerful national agricultural group, with ample members in the local area thanks to still thriving farms.[xv]

In 1953, as some Franklinites finally made their return from the Korean War, which had begun three years earlier in 1950, townsfolk were becoming accustomed to Aldenette, Book Mobile, and Practical Arts services. Almost all of the services inaugurated in 1952 carried over and grew in scope. In fact, 1953, drew hundreds of visitors to an art show put on by adult Practical Arts class attendees.[xvi]

1954 seemed set to blow past records out of the water. Astonishing growth totals hoisted circulation to 45,842—levels never before seen in the library's history. After slow growth in youth circulation, children began to account for a very substantial minority of borrowers, with 15,961 items circulated compared to 29,881 for adults. In some respects, the growth may have been a bit exaggerated. Although the Ray Memorial Association, cooperating closely with the Library Association, continued to fund children's services, the two organizations were realizing that they ought to count both types of circulation in one combined total, given their mutual mission and substantial overlap. Nonetheless, 1954 promised good things in the realm of circulation.

Helen Feeley was positively ebullient about the success of the Book Mobile program, organized by locals. "The Bookmobile service under the direction of volunteers from the Library Association, is now an integral part of work with children through Grade 4, and has built up a tremendous response from children, teachers and school authorities alike. A love of good books and keen interest in reading is being fostered by this co-operation between school and library."

Children were surely excited about something else, too. The Aldenettes donated a high-fidelity phonograph to children's department. Paired with four sets of headphones and a substantial record collection, the phonograph became, "a valuable gift which draws large groups every week to listen to good music and entertaining stories."[xvii]

As 1955 got underway, the lineup of officers changed slightly with the addition of Ruston Lodi as secretary. Taking a look at the gleaming, new phonograph in the children's room, Ray Parmenter, the Association president was one of two phonograph record donors throughout the year.

Meanwhile, the Aldenettes carried on twice-monthly story hours, drawing in kids from 1st through 6th grades. They crowned the year with an outstanding Christmas party for the general public.

The Public Arts group took a fresh approach, giving adults a chance to learn about early American masters and oil painting, exhibiting their work at winter's end in April, 1955. The middle of the decade continued a trend set the year before. Circulation simply continued to grow, edging closer and closer to 50,000.[xviii]

The milestone arrived in 1956 and Ruston Lodi was keen to comment on it. "This is the first year in the Franklin Library in which the total circulation has exceeded 50,000." Throughout the year, the Aldenettes continued to hold story hours and the Christmas Party, as volunteers planned the Bookmobile. However, they mustered extra help from senior Girl Scouts with running each event.

Continuing the repairs started by the Ray Memorial Association, the upper vestibule was redecorated in the springtime, matching the decorative portraits set up downstairs for the Practical Arts show.[xix]

As Sputnik took to the skies above Earth, ushering in the Space Age, Franklinites embraced the decade's growth at the library. Circulation dropped modestly, but remained above 50,000, perhaps as some Franklinites spent more time watching world events and ever-more-popular commercial programming on their black and white television sets at home.

The Library Association gave credit to May Holmes, the chief librarian, and other members of the library staff. Although the staff took center stage, others deserved credit too. The Aldenettes planned their usual programs and topped up the children's record collection with a $150 gift. The year 1957 was highlighted by authors with a connection to the region, three of whom were published throughout the year, including J.H. Feeley, Margaret Page Hood, and Shirley Dana. Their work was well-received by library patrons.[xx]

The year 1959 was one of town savings, thanks to the Library Association's efforts. "Substantial improvements were made on the Library through private funds. A complete furnace was installed, the old railings were replaced with new ones, emergency lights were placed throughout the building, and the electrical system was rewired for extra voltage. These are major expenses for which the Town of Franklin was not burdened." Among the other expenses taken care of by Library Association volunteers, were the costs associated with the Bookmobile service to outlying schools in South Franklin.[xxi]

The '50s were a time of change for Franklin, as the town—and its library association—prepared to reinvent themselves for a community that would grow to proportions never before seen. The money that the Library Association provided -- and saved -- and the investments made in growing and renovating the library laid the groundwork for more change yet to come.

While the Association continued to stretch its resources to meet the growing needs of the public, forces of change were gathering that would eventually help to provide relief. For instance, In February 1955, Massachusetts Governor Christian A. Herter had established a commission to examine the fiscal needs of public libraries. Representatives of noteworthy institutions, including Dr. Paul H. Buck, director of libraries at Harvard University, met to collect facts and statistics regarding public libraries and the activities of the state library extension agency.[xxii] It was a development that portended growing support for libraries from state government in the future.

The following year, The Report of State Aid to Public Libraries, also known as the Buck Report, was presented by the commission. One of its key findings was that the state should provide grants to each public library that met a minimum standard of service.[xxiii] One aspect of this led to an immediate legislative action (in 1959) when the legislature decided that libraries receiving state aid would be required to extend borrowing privileges to holders of cards issued by other certified public libraries. *Not to be outdone, in the fading months of the Eisenhower administration,* the federal budget included $7.5 million for the Library Services Act (the FY 1961 budget). This eventually grew into the LSTA, the Library Services and Technology Act, today the largest source of federal funding support for library services.[xxiv]

While reporting on history decade-by-decade can be arbitrary, there is no doubt that some decades seem to stand alone. The 1960s are a case in point. With a country more prosperous than it had ever been, solutions to the many global challenges as well as those "at home" seemed within reach as the decade began. A new, young, Massachusetts-born President made it even easier to be optimistic locally. However, the high-risk diplomacy of the Cuban Missile Crisis, growing racial strife across the nation, and, of course, the assassination of President John F. Kennedy in 1963, began to change the tone.

The `60s would be a long contest between hope and optimism on one side and grimmer realities on the other. But books and learning were more popular than ever. In 1964, the Franklin Library Association reported a peak circulation of 86,983 books. With Baby Boomers getting into their elementary and teenage years and more people moving to town, the library issued 1,925 new cards and purchased 2,426 books.

By 1964, the library staff had grown to keep pace with these demands. Headed by Dianne DaVia, the head librarian (who resigned on October 29, 1964), the Ray Memorial Library encompassed other staff members including Evelyn Miller (also known as Jean Miller or E. Jean Miller, Betty Swenson, Georgann McDonald, Joyce Adams, Martha Allen, Dianne Danis, Cynthia Di Pietro, and Carol DiMartino.

Throughout the year, Jeanette Harding created floral arrangements and hosted children's story hours, as part of her parallel involvement in the Aldenettes.

While the women's auxiliary participated at the library, the club's main body held their Hobby Show in the library Lecture Room. The Association expressed its gratitude to Raymond Peterson for his frequent contributions of bookmarks, funded by his insurance agency.

The Association extended further thanks to a string of locals who contributed books for the year. And, at the Association, Ray Parmenter surrendered his role as president to Trueman J. Menadue, leaving Edmund J. Keefe in the role of vice-president, C. Lincoln Dana as treasurer, and Ruston Lodi as secretary. The Association also appointed John Goodwin, James Howard and Ray Parmenter as additional officers.

With an eye to another year of expansion, the Association requested a 1965 budget of $30,595.23, with additional funds drawn from the dog tax. Ruston Lodi, who prepared the report, added, "This amount includes a sum from the State which will be returned to the town." [xxv]

Although new library card issuance dropped slightly the following year, in 1965, to 1,881, the Association reported another banner year for borrowing with 2,204 new books added and overall withdrawals up to 92,619. Following her October, 1964 resignation, Dianne DaVia was replaced by Franklin S. Crowther as head librarian. Cynthia and Caroline DiPietro joined the staff, while Carol DiMartino moved on from her post, and resigned along with Christos Georges, Evelyn Miller, and Martha Allen. Frances B. Hunchard also joined as a new participant in library operations.

Reverend Trueman Menadue continued on as president throughout 1965, and the Association retained its same roster of officers.

A new Board of Directors took the helm, along with the officers, spearheaded by George Dana, William Garner, Carlo Geromini, John Goodwin and Marion Holmes, along with Dwight B. MacCormack, Jr.

In place of Raymond Peterson, Benjamin Franklin Savings Bank took over book card donations, while the Aldenettes stayed the course and even expanded their involvement. Jeannette Harding expanded her story time offerings to twice-monthly engagements, between the start of fall in September and the beginning of spring in April.

In contrast with the previous year, Franklin Crowther, the head librarian, prepared the report in place of Ruston Lodi, who was still serving as secretary. He finished his report with a paragraph imploring Franklin residents to employ the library to their benefit, "The Librarian considers the library to be a center of learning, entertainment, self-improvement, and culture for this Town and its environs and essentially a service enterprise. Policies that will improve, increase and extends its service to the public will be initiated and implemented during the coming year as soon as practicable. As a small example there has recently been added a set of books in large print, for the benefit of the partially sighted. Remember, this is your library. Please use it."[xxvi]

The addition of large print books may have been one of the first steps in the direction of the library's present mission of supporting people of all levels of capacity including visually impaired individuals. Franklin Crowther's exhortation to use the library, at the end of the report might speak of the growing excitement in the mid-1960s surrounding other forms of entertainment. Color television—the latest electronic wizardry—had begun to appear in many homes and young people spent free time glued to their "six-transistor" portable radios that blared the latest Top 40 hits.

Fortunately, 1966 brought news of rising circulation and extensive donations, which allowed Crowther to hand the report preparation back to the officers. Lillian E. Duvall, the new secretary, signed off on the report.

Once more, the Alden Club expanded its role issuing certificates for its "Reading for Fun Club," throughout the summer. The year brought few changes in the overall make-up of the group and in total circulation—which rose to 99,090 spread across 9,486 patrons. Adults accounted for the majority of the patrons numbering over 7,000, and also logged the most new library cards issued. Nevertheless, in spite of their smaller numbers hovering around 2,400 patrons, children accounted for over 43 percent of circulation by numbers, even though they made up only a quarter of borrowers.

Donations expanded throughout the year, some new donors supplementing the largesse of regular private donors. There was also support in kind or financial from the American Medical Association, the Embassy of Ireland, Brownie Troop 851, General Tire & Rubber Company, the National Board of Fire Underwriters, and the Seventh-Day Adventist Church.

The only substantial changes to Association membership were the addition of Charles Desaulniers to the Board of Directors and both Donna Streeter and Dorothy Abbott to the staff.

Like Crowther, Lillian Duvall signed off on her report with a hopeful note for the year to come, and recorded, too, a substantial increase in convenience for townspeople. "The Franklin Library looks forward with confidence to continued growth, with expanded facilities and services, to match the growth of the town. It is now open and in service for one-third more hours than before (42 hours at present as against 31 hours last spring). Townspeople in increasing numbers should take advantage of all the many facilities available to them at their public library." [xxvii]

Perhaps color television was not such a terrible nemesis after all!

The year 1967 was the first in which circulation exceeded the magic number of 100,000, actually topping out at 105,085, although the overall number of borrowers remained nearly consistent, climbing only slightly to 11,122. Borrowing a page, perhaps, from the large print books offerings, the library launched a service known as Service to Shut-Ins, bringing books out to elderly residents unable to leave their private homes or rest homes. A person would circulate a regularly updated collection of books within this group of shut-in individuals unable to reach the library themselves. Plans were underway to expand the service or create one in parallel to deliver phonograph records.

The library staff grew, with Barbara George, Deborah Grime, and Eunice Whitman joining along with a new custodian, Stanley Dobeck. The Service to Shut-Ins program was taken on by volunteers from the Alden Club, but in the library's collections a fresh crop of donors contributed material. Among the more unusual donors to the library was the Association of Soviet Friendship, Gaines Dog Research Center, Quaker Oats, President Lyndon Johnson, the Rockefeller Foundation and author, Edward Clark.

Carlo Geromini left his position in the Board of Directors and transitioned to become Vice-President along with Howard Abbott as treasurer and William Carberry as secretary. Besides Geromini's departure from the Board, little changed in its rosters besides the addition of Martin Donahue. William Carberry closed with a typically insistent annual message, finishing in bold terms, reminding residents about accessing the benefits of the library. "To do so, they need only to USE their public library."[xxviii]

The Association tapped its funds more substantially in 1967 than in preceding years, renovating the Librarian's office and the children's stacks and expanding stacks throughout the library. The renewal included a further re-do of the building's aging wiring.
As news of the war in Vietnam, protests, and the first manned-orbiting of the Moon dominated headlines, throughout 1968, library circulation increased by 2000 items, while the makeup of the staff and Association remained relatively static. On staff, Beverly Grime was the only person to join, although the death of William Carberry among the officers and Martin Donahue amidst the Board created great sadness within the organization. Thomas Howard stepped in to replace Carberry as interim secretary, completing the year's report which Carberry did not live to see.

In place of the donors that had provided publications about the Soviet Union, donors now emerged providing books and other items were drawn from new and sometimes relatively exotic sources such as the Minister of Tourism & Information of Turkey, Watchtower Bible & Tract, New England Telephone & Telegraph, NASA, Christianity & Crisis, the Grand Lodge of Masons, the Arabian-American Oil Company and an individual denoted only as "Manny."

The Ray Memorial Board of Directors approved a hefty $1,100 in lighting improvements, which spilled over from the renovations of 1967. Through an aggressive program of card registrations, running to over 325 new cards issued in a single year, juvenile borrowers finally surpassed 3,000 while the Palmer Nursing Home thanked the library for its Service to Shut-Ins program at the other end of the age spectrum.

For the first time, the library began to offer an interlibrary loan program, sharing material with the Audio-Visual Department at Boston Public Library, which helped to sustain a summer film show for preschoolers. Upstairs, in the reference section, Thomas Howard made note of an exceptional number of reference requests, totaling nearly 7,000.[xxix]

In 1969, as the world prepared for a great leap for mankind — Neil Armstrong's historic footstep on the Moon — the library embraced a modern trend emerging at the time: inter-library loan. A service providing this capability to cooperating libraries was established through the Eastern Massachusetts Regional Library System Bookmobile—a predecessor to today's Minuteman library system.

The library marked the loss of Franklin Crowther as head librarian, who passed away on November 20, 1969. Many members remained the same, with the exception of Marion Sampson and Lynne Anderson who each joined the staff. Building on the trends of 1968, children's registrations increased further.

Richard Cairns replaced Thomas Howard as secretary and commented on favorably on donations by Lorraine Metcalf, who contributed a full selection of Town Reports spanning from 1859 through 1968, filling a big gap in library records. Among the year's donors were Franklin Cadette Scouts Troop (with a substantial sum of $928), Leonard Remington, who would later lend his name to the Remington-Jefferson school, and the Thompson Press Company—the factory building by the railroad tracks adjacent to downtown Franklin off of Dean Avenue — replaced only in the last few years by a large apartment complex.

Thomas Howard returned to his commitments on the Board, joined by John Brunelli.
Cairns marked the end of the '60s at the end of his report with an optimistic tone. "It is the permanent objective of the Staff and Directors to broaden the use and usefulness of the Library for all of the townspeople—with the continuing support of the citizens, donors, government agencies, the progress and momentum of recent years can be maintained, and your Library will continue to be a source of civic pride."[xxx]

Chapter 7: The 1970s

The height of the age of sex, drugs and rock and roll may have been unsettling for some, but it proved to be an exciting time for the Association and Franklin Library, as Franklin continued to receive waves of new residents, primarily inbound on I-495, at that point in time a new and largely traffic-free addition to the Interstate Highway System.

Reflecting the increasing role of town taxes in funding the library, 1971 was one of the first years since 1965 in which the head librarian prepared the annual report. In fact, the report was no longer listed as that of the Franklin Library Association, but rather as the, "Report of the Librarian of the Franklin Library." This was a reflection of growing activism from government at all levels – with new federal and state programs starting to provide support for local libraries. In fact, 1972 marked the inauguration of the Eastern Regional Public Library System's daily delivery service for books, media equipment, and information to its member libraries, helping to increase assets available to individuals, even in smaller communities like Franklin.[xxxi]

In contrast to the '60s, circulation and overall borrowers were down. Adult and juvenile circulation levels dropped nearly 10,000 items, hovering only slightly above 100,000 items circulated. Fortunately, the number of new borrowers and cardholders swelled tremendously, doubling for the juvenile category to 661, and surpassing 1,000 for adults.

Arthur Olsen, the new head librarian, reported a display of new adult books during National Library Week and a new book fair during a Children's Library Week. Borrowing an idea from some of the town's youngest residents, film nights were expanded for the elderly. The library had a chance to host Edwin Ribero, a Wrentham-based author who wrote a multi-part history of town agricultural Grange groups.

The growing role of public funding was reflected in library hours. State aid required the Ray Memorial to stay open at least 50 hours a week by 1972. State aid also meant plenty of new statistics and number crunching. The library learned that although average town spending in Massachusetts for books, per person, came out to $0.93. Franklin lagged behind slightly, spending only $0.61 per person. Thankfully, Franklin offset the difference, spending the same percentage as other libraries on supplies, expenses, staff and items. Many new faces joined the library staff including Karol Woo, Lani Desaulniers, Lisa Baci, and Agnes George.

Within the Board, John Fitzgerald, Mrs. J. Parker Vetrano, and Mrs. William Poellmitz joined the group. [xxxii]

By 1973, Arthur Olsen was recording a substantial drop in circulation and falling number of new library card issuance. Juvenile cards fell below 600 issued while circulation dipped to 99,919, falling below 100,000 for the first time since the early '60s. The Ray Memorial Board contributed additional shelves, maintaining a trend begun a few years earlier.

In spite of its greatly expanded hours, the library was not always open and a new book return on School Street helped to handle the off-hours returns.

Breaking a pattern begun in 1968, the Bookmobile ceased to arrive from Charlestown, and instead a different Bookmobile was sourced from Taunton. Dean Junior College, as it was then known, contributed films to Franklin, allowing for a showing of National Gallery of Art films about Impressionist painters in May, 1973. For adults, the Great Books Discussion group intersected with films and Dean offerings, meeting to discuss books every Wednesday night.

The library typically avoided mornings in its scheduling. In fact, Saturday was the only day of the week in which the library opened before 12:30 and stayed open until 5:00. Keeping in mind school and work schedules, the library maintained 12:30 to 9:00 p.m. hours throughout the week and trimmed its hours to 1:00 to 5:00 for the children's room.

In spite of somewhat limited hours for the children's section, local kids enjoyed the benefits of expanded "phonograph" recordings, books and programming funded by the Aldenettes and the Hansel and Gretel Kindergarten, a local business.

Within the organization, Gilbert Dempsey, Mrs. John Brennan, Bernard Albertson and Margaret Murray were among the few new people in the Board, while Chris Cataldo, Cathy Buckman, Mary Ann Dempsey, Marian Naber, Eleaner Pearcey, Elizabeth Sheehan and Jean Bourbeau joined the library staff.

Continuing a trend first set in the early '70s, the town dog officer's report was appended on the page following the library in the town report. Dog licenses were only part of the picture for Alfio Taddeo, the serving dog officer. The 844 dogs he licensed were undoubtedly time consuming, but much of his time was also eaten up by 105 stray dogs killed and buried, 43 Board of Health dog bite reports, 30 kennels licensed and 356 pernicious complaints about dogs. Fortunately for pet owners, 1973 was a better year for dogs than 1971—only 28 dogs had been killed by cars, down from 75 two years earlier.[xxxiii]

Likely of great concern to Arthur Olsen, in 1974, was the year's falling circulation totals. 1973 had been worrisome, with circulation falling below 100,000. Now, it was down even further to only 95,981 in spite of the town's swelling population. New library card issuances, which had topped several thousand a few years earlier fell as well, although there the library was able to report a reasonable total of 1,787.

The Ray Memorial Board undertook a painting project of many of the library's walls and even purchased a locked glass case to protect "valuable volumes," presumably Benjamin Franklin's original donation.

The year's book sale shifted from September to October, while more young children took advantage of library story time.

Within the library itself, the staff split responsibilities evenly. Eunice Whitman led a project to buy more young adult books, catering to the town's swelling teenage population, while Jean Miller loaned out the then somewhat novel cassette tapes, "for use by teachers and parents." Dorothy Abbott assembled a picture collection and Betty Swenson scaled up the interlibrary book and film exchange program.

By the mid-'70s, the library had abandoned its annual list of donor organizations but the librarian continued to recognize some individual and local donors in his annual report. For instance, the Aldenettes along with Ned Keefe were recognized for contributing money to fund new items, and staffer Beverly Grime was applauded for the time she gave to public relations.

The library had many other things to be grateful for. A coin-operated photocopier was soaring in popularity, while a circular provided listings of library holdings and services.

Arthur Olsen keenly called out one favorite patron. "Congratulations to Mr. Joseph Steele, our eldest omnivorous reader!"

In contrast with previous reports, Franklin library was becoming more formal in the way that it defined itself. Library staff were identified by name and position. Betty Swenson, assistant librarian, Hazel Gay, children's librarian, Dorothy Abbott, reference and circulation librarian, Agnes George, clerk, and so forth. The library also boasted four full-time and additional part-time pages, such as Katrina Jaros, Carole Russell, Maureen Malloy, Jean Bourbeau, Mary Ann Dempsey and others.

Olsen closed the year's remarks, reminding residents of the amazing legacy the library provided with a note from the past. "After a visit to the graduation at Dean Academy in June of 1916, former President William Howard Taft wrote in a letter, 'I have never seen a town library equal to that of Franklin. It is a work of art and yet admirably adapted to the real uses of such an institution.'"[xxxiv]

Thanks in part to a Metcalf family donation in the '60s, the library was poised to host meetings of the Franklin Historical Society, which met regularly in its front reading room, flanked by neat copies of past town reports.

With the arrival of the nation's bicentennial in 1976, and the fast approaching town bicentennial in 1978, the winds of change were afoot. Slightly north of Unionville, along Rt. 140, the Tri-County Regional Vocational High School was fast taking shape. The school district reported, "The year 1976 has witnessed the physical emergence of the Regional Vocational Technical School. It is with a great deal of satisfaction that this Committee can finally confirm the fact that the new school will open, as originally planned, in September, 1977."

Simultaneously, Howard Abbott at the Assessor's office was talking with the Computer Study Committee, who wanted to see more examples of the new and emerging technology of computers. Abbott and Lawrence Bassick at the DPW were both skeptical. Both branches of the town government had their own computers, but Bassick did not believe that a central town computer system was called for. "Mr. Abbott stated that the Assessor's Office is completely satisfied with their present system." Abbott insisted that their existing card filing system was all that the department needed.

Even Robert Bell, the Town Treasurer, whose computer service cost the most of all — $4800 a year to run—was disbelieving and saw no challenge in issuing bills the old-fashioned way, with only minimal help from computers.

Up the road, along Pond Street and up into Medway, the Charles River Pollution Control District inherited old town sewage treatment plants, at Mine Brook and elsewhere and footed the bill for a nearly 13-million-dollar construction contract that would see the building of a modern sewage treatment plant to deal with a growing population and serious potential water pollution.

Meanwhile, up at the library, circulation stayed steady at 95,853, similar to 1974 levels, while library card issuance climbed again to 2,082. Charles Desaulniers retained his role leading free film nights, many of them orchestrated at Central Park Terrace.

At long last, Franklin established a full-fledged interlibrary loan program with Dean College library directly across the street. Stanley Dobeck, the faithful custodian, retired in 1976 and Kenneth Harris moved in next door to the library in a house that was later moved from the property.

Abbott, still spearheading the picture gallery, began adding the covers of the *National Geographic* magazines to the walls as decorations.

A number of new, youthful pages joined the staff, including Elizabeth Crockford, LuAnna Breed, Karen LaFrance, Joyce Westin and Pamela Esterley.

With the library as a hub, Franklin scaled up its cultural activities through a specially formed Franklin-Federal Bicentennial Commission. The group sponsored displays in the windows of the Benjamin Franklin bank and showed "Old Franklin" films from the '30s, shot by Stanley Chilson, in the Horace Mann auditorium at Franklin Junior High School (today's Horace Mann Middle School).

By 1979, the annual town report had reverted to a yearly Franklin Library Association report, this time submitted anonymously without the group's secretary or the head librarian signing off on it.

The new report omitted many of the hard numbers that characterized earlier records, but did make note of changes over 1978. "During the year 1979, the circulation of the library increased slightly over 1978." New library card issuance rose slightly but hovered near the levels of the mid-'70s: 2490 new borrowers in total.

The book drop on School Street finally had a name, dubbed the "Reader Eater" by staff. Along with the Aldenette story hour every Wednesday at 10:00 and the Great Books Discussions, the library hosted the Franklin Art Association for oil painting sessions and John Locke, a Dean College professor, who gave travel slideshows once monthly at the Ben Franklin Nursing Home.

Most critically, the Association raised concerns about lack of town funding to complement their continued support, especially after the State Board of Library Commissioners ranked Franklin in the 25th percentile for overall spending and 38th percentile for staff salaries. "Continued taxpayers' support is needed, as efforts abound to minimize the importance of the town library, and consequently reduce the already frugal library budget."

The library greeted the Franklin Art Association with "Welcome, Franklin artists," as the group was invited to make its permanent home in the library. Adding to the aesthetics, the Association purchased 22 new, dark maple shelves.

The end of the '70s brought expectation for the '80s, as Franklin geared up for greater computerization and a rapidly expanding population. However, the end of the decade also brought trepidation. The circulation total recorded for 1979 up to June, 1980 was worryingly low—only 46,067 books in total—a dramatic drop from even the mid-'70s. [xxxv]

A significant development in April 1980, was the signature by Massachusetts Governor Edward J. King on a bill to increase support for state aid to libraries, which had begun modestly two decades earlier. While initially only allocating only $1.9 million to the program, it was a start in a new era.

Chapter 8: The 1980s

By early 1981, the Association and the library staff were able to breathe a sigh of relief. The disturbingly low circulation totals for 1979 and 1980 had finally corrected themselves. Circulation was still lower than it had been in the early '70s, but was back to a more reasonable level of 90,490 books and audio-visual items.

The library retained the hours of operation that it had stuck with throughout the '70s, with the library staying closed on Saturdays in July and August. The book drop, which had seemingly lost its moniker as the "Reader Eater," remained open 24-hours a day, every day of the week throughout the year.

For adults, 1980 and '81 brought a fresh energy crisis, thanks to disagreements with Iran, and a struggling job market reflected the nation in recession. Even though many industries in Massachusetts, particularly in computing and electronics were expanding, the library saw a need to help out adult residents and launched a Geary resume workshop, an outside firm, to help individuals looking for a new job. For children, Children's Book Week was accompanied by a Gerwick puppet show in November.

Lenny and Debbie Gerwick, both aspiring puppeteers, married in June 1974 and had moved into an apartment in Franklin. Debbie had mentioned their plans to the head of the Franklin Library. Interested in doing something special for National Book Week, he hired the pair...and the rest is history [decades later, The Gerwick Puppets are known across the northeast].

In most respects, 1981 was not much different from previous years, maintaining similar hours and circulation as in 1980 and the balance of the '70s. The recently formulated Franklin Historical Commission, which had emerged out of 1970s, collaborated with Franklin Library Association throughout 1981, as the Association made the momentous decision to close the Ray Memorial Library.

The nearly 80-year-old building was suffering from structural problems and the Association feared that its roof would collapse with the arrival of bad winter weather in 1982. As the Commission noted, "The plaster above the book stalls was falling due to a leaking roof." Fortunately, a Boston engineering firm inspected the attic and the roof and announced that the roof would likely survive the winter.

The year 1981 occasioned a major change at the library. Even though the consulting engineers had confirmed that the roof was still intact, it was clear that the library needed major repairs. The Ray Memorial Association, which owned the building and essentially co-managed it along with the town and the Library Association lacked the funds to repair the roof. Instead, they chose to hand over the building's ownership to the town.

Luckily for the library, the Historical Commission had tremendously dedicated members. Commissioner Elizabeth Brunelli personally sought out grants and funds to pay for the repairs, which included new plastering and gutters. The Commission said of the year's work, "We take great pride in our library. It is a magnificent structure for a town of our size and we reject any and all ideas of tearing it down."

The transfer of the library to town hands essentially ended the work of the Ray Memorial Association, and although the moniker Ray Memorial still appears on the side of the building the name began to fall out of favor in reference to the library, with Franklin Public Library being substituted in its place.[xxxvi]

That year, the Franklin municipal offices moved from the old Town Hall (the present Franklin Historical Museum on West Central Street) across the street to the renovated Horace Mann Elementary School (since demolished), The new Franklin town offices were redone in large part by Tri-County students who did almost all of the building's plumbing.

Elsewhere in the downtown, the CATV Committee was hard at work ushering in a new age for the town. Beginning in March, 1980, Franklin launched a licensing process for local cable television. The town went a step further on March 18, 1981, when the Town Council approved a contract with Rollins Cablevision to set up a studio on West Central Street opposite the venerable 1922 fire station.

As Franklinites flocked to the library for summer reading, they also made their way to the newly opened Chilson Beach at Beaver Pond. The Town Pool, which had existed since the 1930s, was finally shut down in 1981 and its location alongside the police station on Panther Way was left abandoned until a 2014 revamp as the Franklin Sculpture Park. Although tight town funds limited the addition of new trees or better services at Beaver Pond, the pond's Recreation Committee looked ahead with hopes of taking over the town dump as additional parkland and ultimately damming up Mine Brook once again to recreate the neighboring Forge Pond which had disappeared after a dam burst in the 1950s.

In 1982, the Town Administrator's report referred directly to the library, describing how the library was managed and largely funded by the Franklin Library Association while the town chipped in funds for heating oil, staff salaries, books, supplies and electricity. However, with the library closed throughout the winter until March, 1982 and the Ray Memorial Association no longer at the reins, change was in the wind.

"The practice of the Town and two self-perpetuating committees, having divided responsibilities for providing a free public library for Franklin citizens, started to unravel..."

The town, now providing the bulk of library expenses and owning the building sought a new agreement with the Association. In turn, the Association reached out to an attorney and drew up a "lengthy and involved" agreement. By assenting to the agreement, the Association gave up its claim to the books, furnishings, library space and other aspects of the library, except for a few remaining offices and a few items given exclusively to the Association, and agreed to begin operating in support of the Library.

The year's library report was issued not by the Library Association but by town staff, who made note of the new situation. "The Franklin Library became a department of the Town of Franklin for the first time in July, 1982. It is under the direct supervision of the Town Administrator, but has no board of trustees. The Town took on the responsibility of administering the Library at least as well as did the Franklin Library Association for a period of 111 years."

When 1983 arrived, the year saw modest circulations again, hovering at 89,235, or as the library director put it, "this figure has settled on a plateau each year since 1978." Gone were the days of rising circulation seen in the '60s, or so it seemed.

While the Bookmobile continued its rounds, coming up from Taunton, volunteers kept children's reading club and the Great Books Discussion group up and running. Meanwhile, the Library Association bought 96 new books, and sponsored passes to the New England Aquarium—the Unitarian Church financed other passes to the Museum of Science.

The new Library Advisory Committee stepped in, headed by Henry Freniere and backed up by Peter Pasquantonio, John Lavigne, Helen Savicki, Lois Russell, John Peters, Cathy Wardwell, Mary Mahoney and William O'Brien and managed to push through additional funds for the 1984 fiscal year. The new funds would cover more books, telephones, additional pages and substitute librarians.

In the library staff, Arthur Olsen retained his role as head librarian, although Beverly Grime, a circulation worker, retired in the fall of 1982. The library stayed tidy thanks to Charles Holmes and Vincent Landi who had taken over from Stanley Dobeck as the new custodians.

In the spring of 1982, a new Library Building Committee was set up, staffed by Woodrow Abbott, Elynor Crothers, Dennis Foley, Allan Karstetter, Nancy J. Rappa, and William Wroblicka to study future expansion of the library.[xxxvii]

The '80s, and the rollout of a larger town government, that now included the library changed the way that the library kept records. Increasingly, the library reported to taxpayers based on the fiscal year. A new approach to running the library meant going by the numbers. As FY 84 got underway, the library conducted a town-wide survey to learn more about its future needs. The results of this survey were used to develop goals for service, collections and staffing.

In contrast with previous years, circulation was up, rising nearly five percent, but reference requests had dropped to 1,955 from highs around 7,000 in the '70s. As Franklin's Cable Commission ramped up local-access television activity, the library bought a videotape player and a color television and began filing videos of Town Council, School Committee and Planning Board meetings.

For popular books, which likely included new novels from the likes of Stephen King, Stephen Coonts and Tom Clancy, the library instituted a book rental program to loan out multiple copies of the same book, simultaneously.

As for the Association, 1983 and '84 were a time to help residents save. The Association bought passes to the Aquarium, Children's Museum, Science Museum and Museum of Fine Arts, which were used 1,493 times—saving residents an astounding $5,932 in admission fees.

Although the Ray Memorial Association had essentially disbanded in 1982, the new state of affairs was made even more complicated by the parallel activities of the Franklin Library Advisory Board and the Friends of the Library. The Friends bought an easel and hosted "Mother Goose programming" for youngsters, while the Advisory Board, the town body set up to advise the library director, hashed out a Mission Statement and new Meeting Room policies.

In the children's department, the first wave of young Millennials were already overwhelming services. In fact, Jean Miller, the children's librarian had to create a story hour waiting list. Meanwhile, Kathleen Pennell set about filming and broadcasting story hours on local access television.

Arthur Olsen and Betty Swenson each retired, and were replaced as director and assistant director by Mary Mahoney and Mary Chute. The only other change to staff was Diane Friend who joined as a part-time library assistant in November.

The Ray Memorial building continued to present fresh complexities, although many of them were resolved in 1984. Court action, in June, finally authorized the formal turnover of the building to the town. Money was put aside for an architectural study aimed at solving the building's space problems, to begin in the 1985 fiscal year.[xxxviii]

More significant changes came to the library in1985, with the town, "continuing to see strong efforts being made to provide quality library service to all and to make the library a visible and viable resource for Franklin's residents." Toward that end, the library expanded summer hours and services and began to open in the morning, during the fall and winter months. Bucking the trend of low circulation begun in the '70s, gains in circulation began to mount, rising over seven percent.

Importantly, even as MTV on cable television drew the attention of young people, young adult circulation skyrocketed by 17 percent. All told, the library was able to boast 9,000 active cardholders and added an additional 1,391 people to the system throughout the year. Twice weekly, the Eastern Regional Library System made book drop offs at the library, keeping interlibrary loan programs up and running, with a total of 200 items borrowed throughout the year and reference requests referred to Wellesley and Boston.

The Friends funded a "West of the Moon" storytelling show, a video club subscription, magazine boxes and an annual book sale as well as a Ray Memorial Birthday Open House, led by the president, Barbara Jarrett. For the first time, the library even introduced a public-use computer, funded in large part by Digital Equipment Corporation. The Association kept up its passes and added new reference material, while its volunteers contributed over 700 hours to the library. The Historical Commission kept up its 'Mini-Museum' in the front foyer, opened in 1984 as an alternative to the town museum on Washington Street.

With the 80th anniversary of the library building, the community reflected on the different groups that helped to keep the library running and commemorated the late Howard Abbott through the Mini-Museum. By now, the Library Advisory Board and Building Committee had fused, selected an architect and submitted a feasibility study to the town which called for an addition and substantial renovations.[xxxix]

Charlotte Ray, the last of the family to be active in the affairs of the library, and library director Mary Mahoney.

As Mary Mahoney put it in her report, "1986 was a year of library successes and accomplishments." The year began with public presentations about the proposed addition and by October 23, 1986, the Town Council voted to support the project.

Hours and circulation expanded at an exciting rate. The library stayed open 58 hours a week and even managed to rise above 100,000 items in circulation, reaching 107,626. Librarians answered an average of 78 reference questions each week, for a total of over 4,000. Interlibrary even double from 1985 totals. With the growing popularity of home video and VCR players, the library finally decided to establish its own video collection, instead of simply borrowing from a video club, a process funded by the Arts Lottery Grant and led by the Association.

Volunteer hours blossomed throughout the year, topping 1000 hours.

At first, town residents seemed a little hesitant to use the new public computer, although 58 people managed to log 494 hours on the machine. Incredibly, much of the circulation—57 percent of it—was accounted for by the children's section.

Although the Library Advisory Board bid farewell to Peter Pasquantonio and Lois Russel, who had served with the committee for four years, they were gripped with anticipation for the upcoming library renovation.[xl]

It would take an intervening year before the addition could begin, but nevertheless 1987 proved to be a fortunate year, as the library received national recognition for being the first public library in the US. A state Board of Library Commissioners grant paid for a microcomputer tapped into the Boston Public Library and Minuteman digital catalogs. The database was already quite comprehensive, allowing access to 800,000 unique titles and over a million items available through a pre-internet online database.

Videos were still sparse in the library holdings, with only 138 cassettes making the rounds 3,662 times. Along with funding computers, the state Library Commissioners encouraged librarians to receive additional training in library science, which Association president, Howard Warcup, set about funding.

In 1987 town expenditures, the library was one of the most substantial, along with over two-million dollars in bonds for renovations—surpassed only by water and sewer bonds.[xli]
With the arrival of 1988, the renovations finally got underway. "During the year, which was frequently highlighted with the pounding of jackhammers and the grinding of drills, many physical changes took place in the historic Ray Memorial Building." The changes included new heating, electrical and plumbing as well as walls and floors torn out to add space. The addition was planned to encompass 6,200 square feet with additional funds from the town that sped up its completion—scheduled for June, 1989.

The library remained open as much as possible through the construction, although library staff and patrons, "learned to adapt to an ever-changing facility." Beginning on November 11, 1987, a human chain of 64 volunteers moved the entire adult collection to the stacks in the Main

Reading Room. All told, 34,000 books changed places in six hours.

By the end of 1989, the Association and the library community were able to enjoy a heartening retrospective on the preceding decade. The library addition had drawn to a close—the new addition had actually turned out larger than originally expected at 6,500 square feet, opening on June 18, 1989. The library had closed entirely for three and a half months during the final and most intense phase of renovations.

Fortunately, in addition to volunteer efforts, state funds amounting to $200,000 had helped to support the build. In spite of occasional service gaps, the library still managed to circulate 65,819 items that year and answered 2,717 reference questions.

Thanks to Assistant Director, Mary Chute, the library procured a $24,000 grant through the federal Library Services and Construction Act to fund elderly programs and services. The new services not only included specialized programming, but also more large-print books and audiobooks on cassette tape, for elderly, vision-impaired readers.

As a result of the addition, the library now offered a large new children's room, better ramp and doorway access for disabled patrons, a redone parking lot, new heating, plumbing and electrical as well as brand new copper roofing.

Simultaneous with other grants, a $7,000 contribution by the state paid for a new microfilm reader and new back issues of newspapers and magazines on microfilm.

As if to signal the growing emphasis on children's services, Marie Fox, the children's librarian, reported 486 kids in attendance for pre-school story hours, throughout 1989 and 351 older children involved in the summer reading program.

The Association dipped into its funds as the renovation project drew to a close and bought new office furniture for the staff, while the Friends launched summer reading awards and the Young at Heart chorus for the elderly.[xliii]

Chapter 9: The 1990s

As Franklin geared up for the 21st century to begin, the library geared up for its own landmark—its 200th anniversary. Henry Freniere, the Chairman of the Franklin Library Board of Directors, spoke of 1990 in glowing terms in his report, but also spoke of emerging challenges. "This has been a momentous year for the Library. In recognition of the Library's unique status as the first public library in the USA, Howard Warcup, President of the Franklin Library Association, chartered a Franklin Library Bicentennial Commission."

The new committee was led by Robert Vallee, from the Town Council, (whose son James would serve as Franklin's state representative from 1994 until 2012).

The Library Advisory Board submitted a proposal in favor of converting to a Board of Trustees, but the proposal was rejected by voters. In the wake of the outstanding library addition, the early '90s heralded budget shortfalls for the library. Nevertheless, the Library Advisory Board remained grateful to the town and its citizens, and appreciative of their support. Freniere wrote, "I feel that I must, at this time, express my warm appreciation to that majority of the Town Council which has supported us and manifested their obvious sympathy. This was evident right up to the hearings prior to the election on the override. Despite the sympathy, there were far too many competing needs to be met to spare the library its devastating cuts following the failure of the override."

Although disappointed about the "Draconian cuts" of 1990, which seemed to threaten service and circulation, the Advisory Board looked fondly at its non-profit associate – the FLA — for their support and congratulated Mary Chute on her succession to the role of Library Director.

Fortunately, chairman John Peters, and other Advisory Board members such as John Lavigne, Nancy Rappa, Elynor Crothers, and Clara Lodi were able to offset the year's setbacks with some outstanding news from the other committees.

Writing on behalf of the Library Building Committee, Freniere discharged the committee's duty and thanked the other committee members including John Peters, Robert Avakian, Henry Strok, Mary Mahoney, Mary Chute and Norm McNeill for their service. After the adventuresome work of building the addition, the committee wrapped up by improving the HVAC system, and repairing damaged paintings in the library, along with memorializing co-chairman Denis Foley, who had passed away.
In preparation for the bicentennial on November 25, 1990, the town had formed the Bicentennial commission in 1988. The group's stated goal became to "promote awareness of the role of the public library in a free society, to promote the Franklin Public Library as a valuable resource to

the community, to promote the 200th anniversary of the first Public Library in America."

The process of celebrating began a year before the formal bicentennial at Dean College and proceeded throughout the year with "colloquia, lectures and concerts."

On November 25, the library hosted music, guest speakers, refreshments, a public get-together and a mock 1790s town meeting, planned by Robert Vallee (who designed a new seal), John Ristaino, Elynor Crothers, and Herbert Hunter.[xliii]

"A year of bad news and good news for the library" — that was 1991. The year started off with budget cuts over the previous year, and eight of the library's 17 employees were laid off, with others receiving reduced hours. Public access dropped from 58 to 20 hours a week, and the allowance for purchasing new items was slashed by 67 percent.

The year marked the first roll-out of the World Wide Web, although early dial-up modem connections a few years earlier had already allowed the library to begin accessing items through the Minuteman digital catalog. Sadly, catalog service was lost throughout the year along with dial-up.

Thankfully, this dry spell in library funding began to take a turn for the better half way through the fiscal year, with the Town Council stepping in with an additional $34,180. Five employees were rehired, and hours climbed back to 43 per week. Even dial-up was restored. Another grant materialized from the federal government for the Literacy Link program—an adult literacy education program. However, the grant was placed on hold for a year until the library was open for more hours. Described as the "brightest spot in the fiscal year," the grant called for hiring a 25-hour per week literacy coordinator.

The new funds were certainly an improvement, but nevertheless the budget shortfall limited library services throughout the year. In fact, in keeping with a state policy of restricting services to libraries with insufficient local funds, the state library commissioners severed Franklin's access to interlibrary loan.

Circulation may have been down to 80 percent of the past year's totals, but reference questions actually increased. Junior story hours were curtailed but volunteers launched four-part puppet shows and schools were invited in during hours when the library was officially closed.

The end of 1990 and the beginning of 1991 were marked by the Persian Gulf War with Saddam Hussein's Iraq. To raise awareness about the events in the Middle East, the Franklin Ecumenical Council hosted "Sand Storms," a series on current events.[xliv]

As the Library Association moved into 1992, the library encountered better news than the previous year. The state library commissioners reinstated interlibrary loan and state aid, although the library accomplished its funding goals only by paring down to 35 hours a week. Even though the library was open for eight fewer hours, residents poured in, raising circulation by nine percent and reference questions by five. On the Ray Memorial grounds, Cub scouts planted trees while Brownies germinated petunias.

An anonymous donation relaunched Science Museum passes and the Franklin Library Volunteers pitched in hundreds of hours of unpaid service in the children's room. An astounding 810 preschoolers took advantage of story times. Children donated small amounts of money to buy new picture books.

The Arts Lottery Council drew in 930 visitors, while 600 children joined the summer reading program. The Friends made up for shortfalls with their twice annual library sales and hosted a competition to decide on a slogan for bumper stickers aimed at raising funds and awareness.

Mary Chute, Library Director, spoke highly of the Association. "The Franklin Library Association proved to be as steadfast as ever. Once again they supported a supplementary book plan which allowed patrons access to bestsellers in spite of the limited book budget." She added, "The dedication of the staff combined with that of the volunteers and other supporters resulted in another exhausting, yet successful year of survival in difficult fiscal times."

Although "survival" and "maintenance" appeared to be the themes of 1992, the year actually brought some startlingly good news. The library reached its highest circulation up until that time, exceeding 131,000 items circulated.[xlv]

Good fortunate finally began to prevail in 1993, with the introduction of a new materials budget, which boosted new books and audio items. Thanks to support from the town and residents, the library finally met minimum public access standards set by the state.

With an eye to fiscal responsibility, a nine-member committee met in September, 1993 to discuss strategic planning and tailoring the library to fit community needs.

As for volunteering, the Library Director commented, "Although no longer as heavily dependent on the efforts of volunteers for basic services, the library and its users continue to benefit from their dedication and enhancement of service levels." Volunteers were critical to the Literacy Link, with 22 involved. Businesses chipped in money for a dozen new magazine subscriptions, passes to Plimoth Plantation and the Acton Discovery Museum, as well as a massive wall map of the globe in the adult section, above the children's room. The map recorded a fast changing and globalizing world, with a united Germany, growing China and quickly disappearing nations like Yugoslavia and the Soviet Union.[xlvi]

The excitement of new technology and growth that were part and parcel of the '90s grew as the middle of the decade arrived. In 1994, the library carried out an automation process, which eliminated the often dizzyingly complex and difficult-to-maintain card catalog. By the end of the year, 30 percent of the collection was barcoded. The Minuteman system trained librarians on how to properly enter data for the sprawling regional system's database. Minuteman was a pioneer in on-line services, and promised to connect Franklin to 29 other libraries, the World Wide Web, and some of the first dedicated websites for a few large library systems, although in 1994, websites still numbered in the hundreds, managed by a few large agencies and universities.

The library community was saddened to part ways with Mary Chute, who resigned and moved to become director of Lynnfield Public Library, after serving as a "jack of all trades," for eleven years, after starting in March, 1984. Susan McAllister was tasked with being interim director, after May, 1994, until Betsy Ferris from Brooks Free Library in Harwich took her place.

Looking back on Chute's service, the library community saw plenty of reasons to be thankful. "Mary had many successes during her tenure as director. She guided the library through difficult budget times, cultivated local citizen support and prepared a long-range plan which set the stage for the library becoming a full member of the Minuteman Network. Throughout her years of service, Mary made the Franklin Public Library a fun and exciting place to work and visit."

The children's room counted record numbers of borrowers, tour groups and a new puppet theatre, while the Northeast Document Conservation Center launched a study in April to preserve the Benjamin Franklin collection. This project was supported by a combination of Franklin Library Association and state grants, which together with $25,000 in donations from business foretold future growth in items and a brighter future for the library's nucleus.[xlvii]

This largesse on the part of the Association was made possible, in part, by a historic decision. At the 1994 annual meeting held on Sept. 27, the membership voted to sell at auction several historic items that it had held which were deemed to be outside of the appropriate scope of the library's collection. These were largely letters written by famous Americans, including Thomas Jefferson. An auction held by Skinner on Nov. 19 yielded proceeds of $47,650 for the Association, which was earmarked for restoration and preservation of the Franklin books and other historic items.

Mary Ferris, better known to her staff as Betsy, began her 1996 report with, "thanks to a fine staff, supportive officials and members of other town departments; to a dedicated Board of Directors under the direction of Clara Lodi, and a most enthusiastic Friends group;
[and] to the Franklin Library Association for its interest in the library, especially the preservation of historical collections; and to the townspeople of Franklin, for a warm welcome and strong community support for the library."

The passing of Dorothy "Dot" Bonney, a longtime library employee, gave a somewhat somber tone to the year. The Friends and the Library Association contributed money toward two CD-ROM workstations in her memory. As Betsy Ferris explained, "Library patrons of all ages have been enjoying new reference sources, such as a street atlas and multimedia encyclopedia, made accessible in easy-to-search CD-ROM format."

Creative minds at the library dreamed up a new way to raise funds. In 1996, a sold-out crowd of 200 watched the play "Murder at the Franklin Library," a mystery drama put on by the Friends. Videos of the play, with all the local "stars" that participated, were available for years afterward in the VHS section.

Meanwhile, in the Literacy Link program, 12 immigrants made their way through a series of three seminars dedicated to the citizenship process, and others enrolled in long-term classes on US government and history.

From Boston, the state library commissioners contributed a substantial grant of $10,000 to support collections preservation. Back at the library, staff raced through the automation process, entering over 80 percent of the collection in the Minuteman system.

As Franklin became part of an ever-growing network, with 32 libraries and 3.2 million items in total, the library's circulation soared reaching 174,661. Thanks to Minuteman, many borrowers from outside the town were accessing Franklin's collections. All told, 5,793 items were requested through inter-library loan. After coming onboard on August 1, 1995, Betsy Ferris played a critical role in the library's transformation to its current form. Following ample training by Minuteman, 1996 marked the first year that Franklin was fully online and connected to the internet, albeit by slower modems and dial-up.[xlviii]

The momentous day came on September 13, 1996, and Franklin has never looked back! Within a few months, Franklin had even more at its disposal, as Minuteman swelled to 37 libraries, five million items, and 640,000 cardholders. 1997 became a race to conserve the past and embrace the future as document preservationists stabilized Benjamin Franklin's books. As Ferris commented, "Franklin patrons have eagerly embraced new features made possible by automation, such as placing requests or renewing items online from their home computers."

The Board of Directors paid close attention to maintenance and accessibility, replacing a cracked, granite lintel above the door frame and installing automatic door openers into the children's section. Like the "Reader Eater" of the '70s, a new free-standing book return was established outside, while the Friends emplaced a photocopier in the children's section.[xlix]

1997 turned out to be another significant milestone for the library. After decades of slowly rising and occasionally falling circulation, the library finally exceeded 200,000 items circulated in a single year, many of them from out of town borrowers. Volunteers powered the library effort, with 2,758 hours contributed.

Growing circulation was certainly tied to Franklin's unprecedented growth, which had started in the '70s and '80s, but reached fever pitch in the '90s. Remarkable numbers of people settled in the town. In fact, witnessing rising traffic levels, the DPW began a process of expanding roads. Rt. 140 would be rerouted and widened, along with segments of Union, Pond, and Pleasant Street.

The tail end of 1997 and the beginning of 1998 brought greater collaboration between the librarians and the Board of Directors. Within the Board, Vicki Coates resigned in September, and was replaced by Enid Gilbert. Taken together, the Board selected Paul Cheli, as Chairperson and Edward Padden as Vice-Chair.

In contrast with the struggles of the early '90s, the library was able to offer expanded hours and services. Hours rose to 63 per week, meeting standards set by the state library commissioners for a community of 25,000. To meet growing demand, Alicia Arsic, Judy Buchanio, Lynn Barry, Anne Fleming, Anita Bennett, Judy Ravinda and Janice Roddy took on extra hours.

Other changes took place in the staff. Library Assistant Wendy Doody changed over from adult circulation to part-time technical services, replaced in her old role by Susan Carlson. Susan McAlister, the Assistant Library Director resigned in the fall, and was replaced by Felicia Oti.

A PhD in library science from Case Western University, Oti had already served as Executive Secretary for the library, and would later become library director. Anita Cook took her place as secretary.

The march of technology continued at the library, with simple changes, such as additional plexiglass for the balcony in the adult section, improvements to the elevator, new security and phone systems, as well as fresh copper gutters. But the big changes were in electronics. Minuteman installed a T-1 phone line for better dial-up service, and a TCP/IP system to get Franklin tapped into the web. The library also broke with old equipment. "Personal computers are gradually replacing the dumb terminals for public access workstations, allowing a graphical user interface for accessing the catalog, periodical databases, and the Internet."

Although the internet was still in its infancy—internet 1.0 — it seemed to be helping with circulation rather than hindering it. Overall circulation was up 18 percent in 1998, and even more in the children's room. "Enthusiastic families," new to town were credited with much of the growth, as summer reading bloomed and story hours swelled with youngsters, many as young as two and a half.

For adults of different national origins, the Library Association played a critical role in supporting the Literacy Link, including funds and an accountant to manage them. Immigrants took advantage of the program to learn English, "needed for survival, [and to reach] to more advanced reading and writing skills." Members of the program hailed from all around the globe: India, China, Peru, Argentina, Italy, Belgium, Russia, Ecuador, Germany and Korea to name but a few.

Nineteen hundred and ninety-eight was a tremendously important year for the Franklin Library Association. Still adjusting to a new role in coordination with the friends and greater connection with the town government, the Association voted to dissolve and shift its funds to the Friends organization. The library expressed its gratitude to the Library Association for more than a century of dedicated service, and to other groups that had made more recent contributions such as the Hunneman Company, Franklin Newcomers Club, and the Lions. Many volunteers were recognized at the annual Volunteer Recognition Brunch, which drew in 160 people.

With Association funds preparing to join the stream of Friends contributions, the library was able to acquire new study carrels, additional museum passes, expand its literacy program and generate "seed money" for additional CDs.[i]

Mary Fox, children's librarian, with some of her young patrons in 1994.

Chapter 10: A New Century

That state of affairs might have seemed to be the end of the Franklin Library Association, but a host of factors conspired to lead to other results. As a volunteer-run entity in a close-knit town, the Franklin Library Association and its sister organization, the Ray Memorial Library Association had been well known to all residents. Their business was the town's business and vice-versa. But as the town grew rapidly and as the municipality itself took on the responsibility for running the library, those two associations moved into a state of limbo. The Ray Memorial Association became effectively defunct, if not formally so, upon the town taking title to the library building in 1981 (formal deeds were filed in 1982 and 1984). Its finances, became mixed and mingled with those of the Franklin Library Association, particularly since some of the same people were involved with both organizations.

As the 1990s advanced, the sentiment had grown within the Franklin Library Association that, absent a crucial role in funding operations and book purchases and given the relatively modest size of the remaining endowment, a future termination should perhaps be considered. And, with a robust Friends of the Franklin Library organization to work with, the intention of gradually passing remaining funds to what was in some ways a kind of successor organization - the Friends — seemed to make sense.

However, the final steps required were complex and involved. Meetings were few and far between and the volunteers that comprised the Association, particularly as individuals retired or got involved with other activities, lost track of the status of the association. Some even believed it had already gone out of existence, though meetings certainly continued into the late 1990s – and an annual meeting in 1997, had supported the concept of dissolution.

But legally, it remained an incorporated entity and its financial resources had yet to be passed on. Crucially, periodic reporting to the Massachusetts Secretary of State had lapsed, in part due to the illness of the treasurer and a misunderstanding of an IRS memo seemingly indicating that regular filing of tax returns was not necessary.

Finally, in 2004, a citizen who served on the Library Centennial Committee (for the Ray building) and the Preservation Committee asked the obvious questions – What is the status of the Franklin Library Association and its remaining funds? — and those questions ended up setting off a rapid-fire series of events which involved officials from the Division of Corporations of the Commonwealth of Massachusetts and ultimately resulted in reorganization and reinvigoration.

Individuals like Ed Padden, involved with both the FLA and the library for many years, were surprised by these developments. Reflecting on that tumultuous period, Padden noted that

FLA members had always stayed in touch informally – bumping into each other in the course of daily life around town. In fact, members were able to quickly locate most relevant financial records from the FLA secretary/clerk and from the treasurer, thereby providing assurances to the townspeople and the authorities in Boston that "the flag was still there" and all was in order. Still, it was not a star-spangled moment. The officials in Boston told the FLA that tax returns might not be required, but annual filing of Form 990, used to clarify the status of non-profit organizations, was required. And, FLA was years behind on meeting this technical requirement.

Plainly the organization needed to dust off its identity and ensure that the mission its founders had given it – supporting the library – was pursued vigorously.

To that end, the treasurer resigned, and, at a meeting of the Association on Oct. 27, 2004, the members agreed to hire an attorney and CPA to review records and procedures to ensure all was proper. Banks and other financial services firms holding FLA monies were queried to make sure all relevant records were taken in hand. In fact, over the period in which reporting had lapsed, the market value of the accounts had increased from $180,459.22 to $239,336.85. Checking accounts and certificates of deposit held in a local institution had also risen.

All of this took a tremendous commitment of time for members, particularly Ann Whelan who had previously served as treasurer and was now asked to serve as "acting" treasurer. With so much tumult, the notion of disbanding now seemed unwise, since it might convey the impression that the organization had failed or been driven out of existence. In fact, its heart was still beating strongly and long-time director, Henry Freniere, called for an annual meeting, the first formal annual meeting in several years, for January 12, 2005. Deliberations and meetings became more regular.

At a June 26 meeting attended by Vicki Buchanio, Elynor Crothers, Henry Freniere, Clara Lodi, Ed Padden, Ann Whelan, and Mary Jane Whiton, the association acknowledged the receipt of $4290 in memory of Doris Abbott, a long-time library volunteer. Whelan reported on her efforts to get a professional to prepare the IRS Form 990 for the organization. Significantly, she also let the members know that she had found a potential replacement; Armand Fernandez, an assistant vice president at locally-headquartered Benjamin Franklin Savings Bank.

Fernandez, who had attended a seminar for non-profits, recommended that the association implement changes such as requiring two signatures on checks, acquiring use of a safe deposit box for important records, adding a vice president to the association roster and bringing in new members. "A treasurer is not a financial planner," he noted, yet, with investments in a dozen different funds and no specific operating strategy, a plan was needed. Furthermore, based on its original charter, there needed to be legal clarification of what purposes could be supported by the Association. Crothers, for one, recommended refocusing on preservation. Finally, Fernandez suggested, inventorying all the documents and items held by the association and finding records that may have gotten scattered. Buchanio, reference librarian for the town, volunteered to dig into the files at the library to see what could be uncovered.

When the same group met again in September of 2005, this time joined by Robert Brown from the Friends, library director Felicia Oti, Barbara Smith, and Kenneth Weidemann, they had Fernandez in attendance, too; a person whose financial experience would be an asset to the organization moving forward. And, after a brief discussion, they voted to bring him aboard as both a member and as treasurer. The appointment also relieved Whelan of the responsibilities she had unexpectedly had to take on a year earlier. Freniere was able to report that the law firm of Gilmore, Rees & Carlson was working on designation of the FLA as a public charity and preparing a mission statement and other documents needed to comply with current state requirements. Brown resigned his seat in favor of Oti, further strengthening the ties of FLA to the library.

Continuing to strengthen the organization for its renewed mission, Scott F. Nolan, a public servant with strong knowledge of compliance matters and understanding of non-profit organizations, was recruited by Fernandez and elected president in September of 2006. Other important organizational steps followed, with a vote to formally certify a board of directors the following month.

Over the winter, the preservation agenda began to take shape. In April of 2007, Nolan wrote to Oti inquiring about preservation needs and opportunities for the original books donated by Benjamin Franklin as well as other historic items and library features such as paintings.

At that month's meeting, Nolan provided an update on progress with getting back in good standing with the IRS and efforts to get guidance from the state on handling funds with restricted purposes that might now be moot. As Padden explains, the FLA founding fathers never envisioned the needs of a modern library with computers, DVDs, and online resources.

Nolan also noted the need to avoid any appearance of conflicts of interest involving the library and suggested that library employees on the board simply abstain from voting on matters relating to the library. Oti, for her part, used the meeting to request funds from FLA to cover preparation of custom glass doors to protect old and fragile books.

Renewal of FLA's non-profit status with the IRS finally came in August of 2007. The upshot of that determination was that FLA was treated as a foundation rather than a charity, meaning it was not required to actively raise money, merely to make appropriate disbursements in the best interests in preserving the library and the community.

But all the problems and uncertainties would not be resolved overnight.

One, looming issues, was management of the endowment funds, many of which were positioned in "growth" investments that had performed well in recent years but represented a higher risk. Padden recalls that Nolan and Fernandez were strongly in favor of moving toward a mix of less-risky investments. And, over a period of several months, with the support of the directors, they accomplished that change.

It was fortuitous, because markets grew more volatile in 2008, culminating in a series of downturns that destroyed billions of dollars in value globally. Nolan and Fernandez refuse all claims of prescience and insist they were just acting as any trustee should but the result of their move was that the FLA's funding was scarcely disturbed by the Great Recession, as the period came to be known, leaving the organization in a good position to carry its mission forward. It was also, Nolan notes, a new era of transparency where everyone involved had visibility into the location and purpose of investments and bank accounts.

The library itself, was not so fortunate in that period, though. Town finances took a big hit as the economic slowdown spread across the nation, and a large layoff of staff was implemented in 2010 along with a general tightening of the budget.

Nolan and Fernandez were eager to help the library with both preservation and new technologies, though Padden admits he was among those anxious to ensure absolute clarity about the FLA's ability to disburse funds in those directions.

On the human side of the FLA, three long-time members passed away in that first decade of the new century. Barbara Smith was the first, passing away in 2006, Henry F. 'Hank' Freniere Sr. 90, departed late in 2009. Clara M. (Dwinell) Lodi, 84, followed in April of 2010.

The ongoing role of the FLA in the town and within the library community remained unclear to many, however. For example, according to Nolan, the FLA made a donation to the library of $15,000 with certain restrictions on its use. But whether those restrictions were respected was not clear. Subsequently, a representative of the library board visited with the FLA and took the position that the library board should "call the shots" and the FLA should provide funds as requested; a position Nolan, Fernandez, and the board felt was at odds with their fiduciary duties under the original charter and the revised recognition of the FLA's status as a foundation. That position was further strengthened in 2013 when consultations with an outside attorney focused on foundation issues clarified case law and practice around the duties and rights of trustees relative to "original intent" and the reasonable interpretations that might need to be made regarding appropriate modern uses of monies.

But the FLA was still seen as a potential target by others. For example, the town administration also made a forceful case for simply turning over the remaining funds to the town for management or disbursal. But mindful of the struggles the FLA had originally initiated to simply make the town's public library a reality in the 19th century, and all the long decades of perseverance that followed, the members saw no reason to submit. And, in the end, comity returned and the town, the library, and the FLA acknowledge their respective spheres of action.

Finally, it seemed, the FLA could focus on its primary final goal: preserving and protecting the legacy of the Rays and the founders and supporters of the library over the centuries past.

In 2016, with the library again in the midst of a massive expansion and renovation, that preservation mission rose in prominence. The town Library Building Committee also expressed strong interest in making sure historical features of the building were not only protected but, if possible, restored during the renovation and the notion of not only preserving but actually exhibiting the Ben Franklin collection also surfaced. At the request of Building Committee Chair, Judith Pond Pfeffer, the FLA expressed a willingness to support the construction of a special display case. Pfeffer took the lead and developed a design with a company specializing in museum displays. And, the FLA duly provided the requested support, with the case installed and the books unveiled to the public in April 2018.

Chapter 11: The New Library Addition in Process, 2017-2018

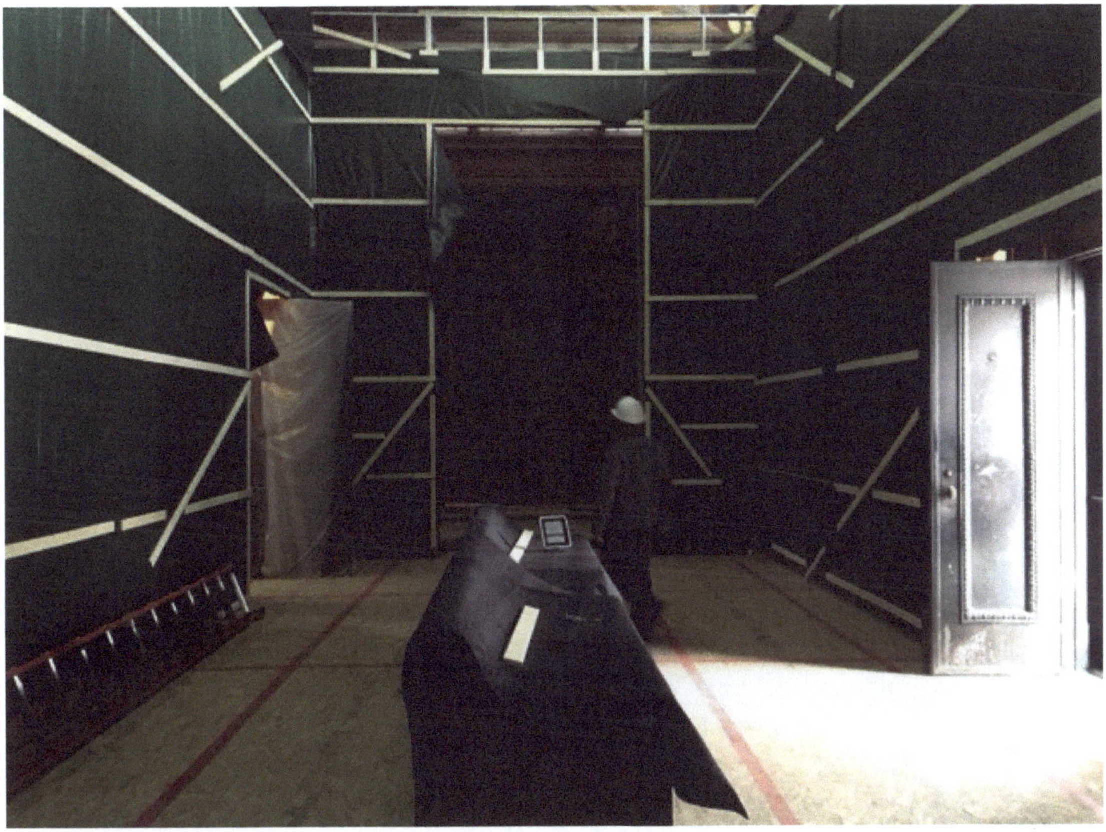

Courtesy of Maria Lucier

Courtesy of Maria Lucier

Courtesy of Maria Lucier

Courtesy of Maria Lucier

The addition completed in 2018

Paul Vicario

Paul Vicario

Paul Vicario

Paul Vicario

Paul Vicario

Chapter 12: Citizens Quarantined and the Library Locks its Door: Coronavirus 2019

With the library addition complete, the display case for Franklin donated books completed, and other preservation projects moving ahead, it seemed like "smooth sailing" for the FLA–supporting preservation in the near term and then, in an orderly fashion, making final disbursements and closing the books for good, with a target of 2022, the 150th anniversary of the organization's original incorporation.

But as the second decade of the new century drew to a close, life in Franklin and, indeed, everywhere in the world, was rapidly changed by perhaps the greatest pandemic since the influenza epidemic of a century earlier.

On March 3, 2020, the Massachusetts Department of Public Health (DPH) announced its first presumptive positive case of COVID-19 since testing started Friday, February 28, at the State Public Health Laboratory. The woman so diagnosed was in her 20s and lived in Norfolk County. She had recently traveled to Italy. a hotspot on the global infection map, along with a school group and was symptomatic.

Coronaviruses are respiratory viruses and are generally spread through respiratory secretions (droplets from coughs and sneezes) of an infected person to another person. Symptoms of COVID-19 include fever, cough and shortness of breath, and, in severe cases, pneumonia (fluid in the lungs) and death.

With the contagion spreading geometrically, states, including Massachusetts, undertook unprecedented lockdowns of schools and businesses, and even libraries.

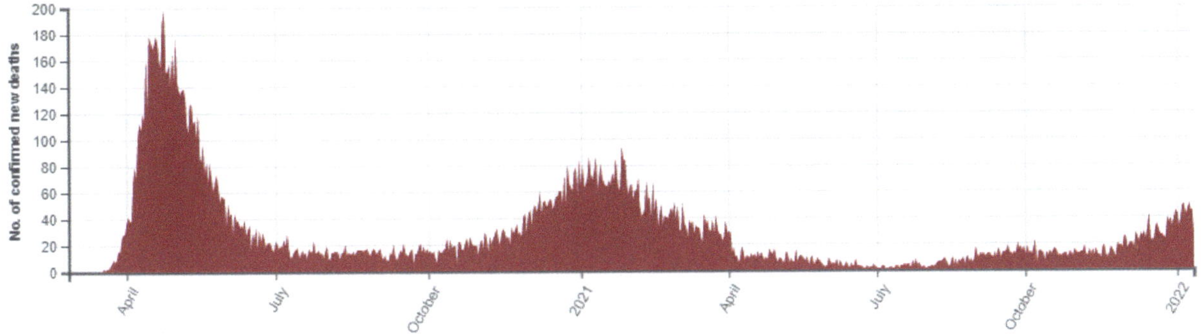

Massachusetts Covid Deaths Per Day (Wikipedia)

Perhaps unsurprisingly, this crisis called for fresh thinking within the Franklin Library Association. Books, learning, culture and preservation had to be addressed, but people were dying and many suddenly faced a shortage of basic necessities.

Urged to action by FLA President Scott Nolan, the Association agreed that extraordinary times demanded extraordinary measures, and authorized a disbursement to a local social agency, the Franklin Food Pantry.

It was a timely gesture, which earned the appreciation of the Food Pantry.

FRANKLIN
FOOD
PANTRY

April 27, 2020

Franklin Library Association
430 Franklin Village Drive
PMB#300
Franklin, MA 02038

Dear Friends,

On behalf of the Franklin Food Pantry and the families we serve, please accept my heartfelt thanks for your generous gift. During this unprecedented health crisis, your support is needed more than ever.

Your support helps the Pantry serve more than 1,100 individuals in need each year and we expect those numbers to grow as we see the long-term impact of school and business closures take effect.

Your gift helps us purchase fresh and nutritious foods such as chicken, beef and other meats, dairy products, eggs, fresh vegetables and fruits. Because of you, our families will have access to enough food so they do not go hungry.

Thank you again for remembering the Franklin Food Pantry.

Sincerely,

Lynn Calling
Executive Director

Your donation of $10,000.00 made on 04/22/2020 is a charitable contribution. No goods or services were received in exchange.

Learn more about helping our efforts to end hunger in our community. Please subscribe to our newsletter on our website and/or follow us on Facebook.

Tax ID #04-3272663

Relieving hunger. Nourishing lives.

Then, as lives and libraries began to return to some semblance of normal, an opportunity to enhance the library with an interpretive display emerged, focused on the important role of the Library's key benefactors.

Chapter 13: Sisters in Philanthropy

While the bedrock importance of the whole Ray family, particularly the men of the family who built its fortune and shaped the town and the region, has been mentioned numerous times in this book, special mention needs to be accorded to two Ray women.

Above, the painting of Emily (Rockwood) Ray and Joseph Gordon Ray, Jr. at the library.

Lydia P. Ray and Annie Rockwood Ray were born in 1854 and 1856, respectively, to Joseph Gordon Ray, Jr. and Emily (Rockwood) Ray. By all accounts the pair seem to have had the deepest affection for their parents and, in an era when women still had limited rights and opportunities, constrained by tradition, they both pursued education and lives of active engagement. Both were involved with the arts and culture as well as with a wide spectrum of good works on behalf of the Franklin community and many individual inhabitants.

Both women attended and graduated from Dean Academy and Lydia went on to complete studies at Vassar College in Poughkeepsie, New York, the second degree-granting institution for women in the United States. And, while both pursued similar interests, Lydia, perhaps due to her long association with Dean, seems to have achieved more public notice than Annie.

Vassar in its early years gained particular notice as the home of world-famous American astronomer, librarian, naturalist, and educator, Maria Mitchell, who discovered a comet in 1847 later known as "Miss Mitchell's Comet." The pioneering female scientist would have been an important presence at Vassar in the years when Lydia studied there.

Although Vassar today carries a hint of privilege around its name, historians of the institution note that its early students were more likely to come from the "rising middle class" rather than the truly rich, whose daughters were often sent to Europe with personal tutors.

As noted elsewhere, Lydia married Professor Arthur W. Peirce, at the Ray family's Elm Farm in June of 1903. Some 150 guests gathered from across Franklin and across the nation. Arthur W. Peirce ("AWPie" was his informal nickname at Dean, where he taught) seem to have shared broadly, Lydia's interests and as far as one can tell from the relatively sparse records, did not interfere with his wife's interests or charitable activities.

Lydia was a member of the Bibliophile Society of Boston, which described itself as having been formed "for the purpose of the study and promotion of the arts pertaining to fine book making and illustration, and to the occasional publication of specially designed and illustrated books for distribution among its members at a minimum cost of production."

The books published by the society were from a wide range of ancient and modern literature such as *Border Ballads* (1912) and *Charles Dickens* and *Maria Beadnell: private correspondence* (1908).

A 1923 Vassar publication mentions that "Lydia Ray Pierce's (*sic*) husband was seriously ill during last summer, but recovered in time for them to spend the latter part of the vacation in Maine as usual." This was very likely Poland Springs Resort, where many other well-off New Englanders spent time in the summer season. The lovely gothic revival All Souls Chapel was built in 1912, with the two-year old grandson of former vice president, performing the ceremonial ground breaking. In 1916 the chapel received the addition of a stained-glass window, the Ray Memorial window, honoring Emily R. Ray and Joseph G. Ray. It was a gift of Lydia and Annie and in a triptych form that illustrates the parable of the Good Samaritan. It was created by the Gorham Company of New York City, a competitor to Tiffany & Co. at that time.

A writer in a 1929 Vassar publication mentions encountering Lydia Ray Thayer and another classmate of 1878 while visiting Nantucket.

The class notes section of the Vassar Quarterly for July, 1934, notes Lydia's absence:
"It was announced at the alumnae luncheon that the cup for the largest percentage of members in attendance had been awarded to the Class of 1878, so for a second time we have won this honor. Those present were Harriot Stanton Blatch, Helen Brown, Fanny Littlefield Capron, Sarah Louise Day, Mary Hubbard, Marie Ives Humphrey, Harriot Ransom Milinowski, Martha Hillard MacLeish, Laura Brown Smith, and Annie Pidgeon Searing. Four more had planned to be present —Mary Clarke Acker, Jennie Davis, Lydia Ray Peirce and Margaret Pierson —but were unable to come on account of illness."

Then the Vassar Quarterly of January 1937, noted, 'Lydia Ray Pierce (*sic*), '78's "dear Lyddie," has joined those who are our most beautiful and precious memories. After a long period of semi-invalidism, the sudden death of her husband, two or three years ago, was a shock from which she never fully recovered. She died in Franklin, Mass., in her old home, on December 18th. Her whole life had been bound up with Franklin Academy (sic), of which her husband had become headmaster. Always over-modest in estimating her own fine qualities, over-generous in judging others, gentle and gracious in all her ways, Lyddie held a place peculiarly her own in the hearts of '78. Not one of us who remain but feels the poorer for her passing.

A detailed encomium in Dean's official magazine further lionized her memory and made particular mention of her beneficence toward Franklin.

"Mrs. Peirce was interested in every civic betterment, and every good cause in the town had her support and financial aid. She was an active member of the District Nursing Association and through this channel did considerable charitable work. The Ray Memorial Library and the Ray Science Building at Dean, other gifts of Mrs. Peirce and her sister, Mrs. Annie Ray Thayer, for the improvement of the town, stand as testimonials of her great interest and generosity in this direction..."

Not all Lydia's gestures were large. In 1908, noticing that the children attending the town's one-room school house – the Brick School – had no play yard because the building occupied nearly the whole site, she took steps to acquire a lot adjacent and behind the school and equipped it as a playground.

Dr. Marvin, her pastor at Grace Universalist Church on the Dean campus, also offered fulsome praise.

"We remember her unfailing sympathy and tact, her unobtrusive coming and going on errands of love and mercy. she went the rounds of our town to people of all classes, creeds and conditions. Her horse and carriage and veteran driver, with her bountiful basket of good things, have been a familiar sight on our streets, rain or shine, these many years. The best part of her giving was that she gave herself with her gift. She never forgot her friends. She remembered their birthdays, even as they came in an annual rotation. Such lives make it plain what the Master meant when he spoke of his second coming. it is said that Stanley knew there was a Christ when he knew there was a Livingstone. Some of us have found it easier to believe in Christ since we have known this Christian lady."

Annie, of course, was also active in many ways throughout her life. For instance, as a prominent supporter of Franklin Square House, in Boston. Located in the South End, it was founded by Reverend George Perin, who was concerned about the conditions facing single, working women in Boston who could only afford to live in the poor-quality housing in the most dangerous neighborhoods. Perin was not wealthy, but he was resourceful and tirelessly raised funds until he was able to purchase the Franklin Square House in 1902 to meet the needs of "women adrift" — with shelter, food, a safe place to socialize. Known as "The House that Love Built." Franklin Square House became.

[More recently, in 1970, the house was sold to the city, becoming the new Franklin Square House, providing housing, shelter, and day care services for battered women.

Confined to her home by illness starting in May 1935, and cared for by her sister, she nevertheless outlived Lydia, passing away in 1944.

Described by the *Sentinel* as a "A woman of dominant personality, the years of her activity knew her generosity and benefactions in town and wherever her interests centered.

She married Adelbert D. Thayer of another prominent Franklin Family and were reputed to enjoy hunting and fishing together in Maine. They later shared a summer home in Orleans on Cape Cod.

Together with their husbands, the sisters made two trips around the world. The sisters were also famous for their adjacent homes opposite the Dean Campus and adjacent to the library they had built.

At her funeral, Rev. Trueman J. Menadue, pastor of the Grace Chapel, lauded her lifetime of generosity and read "Transfiguration," a poem by Louisa May Alcott

Mysterious death! who in a single hour
Life's gold can so refine
And by thy art divine
Change mortal weakness to immortal power!

Bending beneath the weight of eighty years
Spent with the noble strife
of a victorious life
We watched her fading heavenward, through our tears.

But ere the sense of loss our hearts had wrung
A miracle was wrought;
And swift as happy thought
She lived again -- brave, beautiful, and young.

Age, pain, and sorrow dropped the veils they wore
And showed the tender eyes
Of angels in disguise,
Whose discipline so patiently she bore.

The past years brought their harvest rich and fair;
While memory and love,
Together, fondly wove

A golden garland for the silver hair.

How could we mourn like those who are bereft,
When every pang of grief
found balm for its relief
In counting up the treasures she had left?--

Faith that withstood the shocks of toil and time;
Hope that defied despair;
Patience that conquered care;
And loyalty, whose courage was sublime;

The great deep heart that was a home for all--
Just, eloquent, and strong
In protest against wrong;
Wide charity, that knew no sin, no fall;

The spartan spirit that made life so grand,
Mating poor daily needs
With high, heroic deeds,
That wrested happiness from Fate's hard hand.

We thought to weep, but sing for joy instead,
Full of the grateful peace
That follows her release;
For nothing but the weary dust lies dead.

Oh, noble woman! never more a queen
Than in the laying down
Of sceptre and of crown
To win a greater kingdom, yet unseen;

Teaching us how to seek the highest goal,
To earn the true success --
To live, to love, to bless --
And make death proud to take a royal soul.

The bearers, with names long attached to her family and its works, included Dr. D Thayer Gallison and his son, Pf. Davis T. Gallison, and Robert E. Thayer as well as Earle S. Wallace, Alexander C. Ewen, and Joseph E. Bourret.

* * * * * * * *

It took much more than a century, but finally, the women benefactors who actually made the Ray Memorial Library a reality – sisters — got formal recognition at the library, in the form of a handcrafted mahogany pedestal and a modern kiosk and slideshow installed in 2022, with support of the Franklin Library Association, facing the Main Street entrance.

FLA member Nancy Rappa had long been bothered by how little library patrons and people in Franklin in general knew about Lydia and Annie. So, she proposed to do something about it, convincing her fellow FLA trustees to support an interpretive exhibit researched and authored by Reference Librarian Vicki Earls.

The final partner in the project was Rocco Cavallaro, a Franklin-based craftsman, sign maker, and a passionate worker of wood. With cues from Rappa and Earls, he laboriously built a pedestal of solid mahogany, even incorporating design motifs from the library and the Ray family crest. That was topped, literally, with a built-in screen with PowerPoint slides created by Earls that displays the story of the Ray sisters, finally making them an integral part of the library.

"I'm so thrilled that this if finally done," said Rappa. "It's long overdue," she added.

Above, Vicki Earls, Rocco Cavallaro, and Nancy Rappa — the team that brought the story of the Ray Sisters back into the library through a new display kiosk. (Franklin Observer, 12-22-2021)

Similarly, as the year of the 150th anniversary, 2022, came around, the leadership of the town took notice. Again, as reported in *Franklin Observer*:

The Town Council honored the Association and its current president, Scott F. Nolan, for all those generations of support and, in particular, for recent largesse totalling some $65,000, being applied toward preservation and restoration of the artwork in the historic library building along with some of its most irreplaceable contents.

Responding on behalf of the Franklin Library Association Board of Directors, Nolan said it had been a "privilege and an honor to work with [library director] Felicia and her staff, with Jamie Helen, and with many other people over the years." He also acknowledged the leadership of his many predecessors as president of the Association and mentioned the Ray family and other early leaders who set the library on a positive path, particularly with the completion of the Ray Memorial building in 1904.

Above, Scott F. Nolan, President of the Franklin Library Association accepts the commendation of Town Council Chair Tom Mercer as Library Director Felicia Oti (center) looks on. (Screen Capture from Franklin TV)

By choosing to continue operating, the Franklin Library Association has dedicated itself to the continuation of public library service in the town of Franklin, proceeding far into the future. But what place does a private association and a public library have in the future?

During the final years of the 2000s and the start of the 2010s, popular media made great fanfare about the death of print. At the time, it seemed as if books were fast disappearing, and many fans of the printed word looked glumly into a future digital dark age, dominated perhaps by too many games of Candy Crush, Call of Duty, and Angry Birds.

Nevertheless, libraries continue to grow and thrive. Ironically, in an age where digital technology has risen to the forefront, libraries are growing at an astounding rate. Just as the 1980s witnessed the rise of the Minuteman Library System and similar regional systems like C/WMARS and SAILs, so to have the 1990s, 2000s and 2010s witnessed startling expansions at many libraries—including the Franklin Public Library.

For once, local governments are finally able to fund culture, education and recreation through public institutions such as libraries. However, even in this new-found world of arts, culture and public institution grants, funds can still be very tight for libraries.

As one library commentator put it, just as elevators are no threat to stairs, neither is the internet a threat to books. Thanks to the internet, library patrons are now able to tap into outstanding interlibrary loan programs offered through the Minuteman system, which allow borrowing as far away as Natick, Framingham, and Cambridge. Through the same system, Franklin residents are now able to tap into outstanding college libraries, including Dean College's library opposite the Ray Memorial building on Main Street.

Simultaneously, patrons now have access to WorldCAT. Although the system might conjure images of an overly large feline, the name is actually a shortened version of World Catalog. Essentially, WorldCAT combines elements of our regional library system, but extends it across thousands of libraries and library systems around the globe. Today, it is possible to find out the availability of items around the world and even order them through special requests. Items can ship from as far away as Nebraska—or Australia.

As ever, the library's greatest strength is its books, but today more than any time in the past the library extends beyond simply, "books, papers, collections in natural history and works of art." Today, collections really is plural, with patrons enjoying access to thousands of books, DVDs, Blue-Ray discs, video games, CD-ROMs, encyclopedias, dictionaries, online databases, and local history rooms. This extensive laundry list of modern advantages ignores the equally substantial benefits from public programs, such as children's events, performers and guest speakers.

In the future, libraries such as Franklin Public are apt to enjoy even greater variety than they do today. Some libraries have adopted tool exchanges and massive digital holdings in the form of e-books and reports. Expanded, diversified services will play a leading role in the future of the library, backed up by guidance and funds from the Franklin Library Association.

Taking center stage at the future Franklin Public will be the Ray Memorial Library building, which completed its third phase of renovations since 1988. This transformation will allow the library to adapt for future demand, while sustaining its historical architectural and artistic beauty.

With a population expected to hover around 40,000 people, Franklin will welcome a diverse community of both settled and transient families, seeking a place to go to meetup and tap into their community. Franklin Public Library will fill this role, long into the future. and Franklin Public Library will continue to rely on donations, philanthropy and the public spirit of dedicated supports that will succeed the Franklin Library Association in the years to come.

As the most fearsome months of the Covid pandemic faded from view, the library gradually got back to its routine. Even the rhythm of the FLA's periodic meetings resumed.
In the final months of its existence it continued its support for the preservation of the library—both the visual elements of the library and the historic paintings that hang on its walls but also irreplaceable documents in need of digitization and preservation.

As in the days of Oliver Dean and the Ray family, the Association sought to honor the past and the treasures, tangible and intangible, associated with the library and the Association, while pointing to a positive future for Franklin and its citizens.

Afterword

The Franklin Library Association was founded on October 7, 1872; a group of prominent men with a mission to serve the public while following Ben Franklin's advice in his letter to the townspeople, 'sense is preferable to sound,' laid the foundation for establishing the first public lending library in the new nation.

I was elected President of the Franklin Library Association (FLA) at the Annual Meeting on September 18, 2007. It was a tumultuous time over 15 years ago as the board collaboratively sharpened its focus on preservation and established financial practices transparent to an actively involved board that was committed to preserving this historical treasure: our library. In leading this board through many milestones with the first being, to build a collaborative partnership with the town, as the FLA moved steadily to restore paintings, preserve historical documents, and purchase the custom library cabinet that stores the books Ben donated to the towns people.

Then, FLA supported the custom cabinetry skills of Rocco Cavallaro, working with Nancy Rappa (FLA) and Vicki Earls (Franklin Public Library), to envision the explanatory pedestal with the carved representation of a book, now in the `delivery room' of the library as well as and the hand-crafted cabinet in the front entranceway with the electronic history of the library. These two items are a testament to the history of the library that must be preserved for future generations. These pieces are also a physical tribute to all the members of the Franklin Library Association over the past 150 years. They served, selflessly, to honor the contributions of the Ray family – who built and endowed the Ray Memorial Library, to the town. They volunteered their time and energy to carry forward a mission to preserve the historical books, the building, and artifacts of Franklin's unique history.

I am humbled to have served and been surrounded with the board members whose families go back many generations and whose love of Franklin are reflected in this historical book. My wish for those who read this book is that they find a sense of wonder and curiosity reflected in the library's history, while taking a moment to reflect on the importance of service to one's community. This is what I believe is the message of the Ray family and is true today in all our modern activities and in our service to others in the community.

There are so many people to thank, however I must attribute my first visit to a public library, the desire to learn and to become an educator, to my late mother, Patricia M. Nolan.
The past fifteen years has been an amazing journey as we close the last page in tribute to the Franklin Library Association.

Scott F. Nolan
President, Franklin Library Association
October 1, 2022

Town of Franklin

355 East Central Street
Franklin, Massachusetts 02038-1352

Phone: (508) 520-4949
www.franklinma.gov

Office of the Town Administrator

February 2, 2022

Franklin Library Association
430 Franklin Village Drive, PMB #300
Franklin, MA 02038

Dear Franklin Library Association,

On behalf of the Town of Franklin, I would like to thank you for your extraordinarily generous donation to the Franklin Public Library. Your continued and ongoing support of our library has funded several important initiatives over time, and this most recent donation will allow us to preserve and digitize seven historical manuscripts and restore several murals in the Delivery Room. The Town of Franklin is extremely fortunate to have your support.

We cannot thank you enough for your generosity and for choosing to give back to our community. Please do not hesitate to call if I can ever be of assistance.

Warmest Regards,

Jamie Hellen
Town Administrator

cc: Felicia Oti, Library Director

Scott, what more is there to be said?..
We are forever grateful.

Appendix A: The Franklin Library Association Register, 1872-2022

This leather-bound tome, purchased from Charles K. Darling-Blank Book Manufacturer in 1872 has served as the Franklin Library Association's main written record of members since that time. In fact, entries are still being made in the same book, with additions to the Register right up to the present day. It is rare for one organization to have such an enduring legacy in a single volume—although as the Franklin Library Association celebrates over 150 years of operation, such a Register is useful for organizational history and helps to underscore the group's long-standing and continuing legacy.

The following passages are transcribed directly from the Register to guarantee the survival of crucial information about the Franklin Library Association's past as the group moves deeper into the 21st century.

The Register begins with an account of members serving at the time of incorporation in 1872, many of whom had participated in the group's initial work as far back as 1858. These early names are a strong account of Franklin as it was in the 1870s—many surnames reflect a British origin, such as Rockwood, Ray or Makepeace, while others were likely descended from French Huguenot stock.

Many of the families that are now associated with Franklin 'townies' had yet to arrive in the community, as families such as the Sullivans, Daddarios, Padulas, Vallees, Vendettis, and others had not yet immigrated to the US or were playing a smaller role in Franklin's community. It seems virtually everyone of note in 1870s Franklin signed on to the Library Association.

A large gap exists in the Register between 1872 and 1915. A subsequent clerk or Association member updated the Register in the margins, writing in pencil, noting the fate of early members—many of whom had passed away or moved away by the time of his or her writing.

We the undersigned serving life members of the Franklin Library association Established in Franklin, December 22, 1858, for the purpose of perpetuating the Same and Extending its usefulness, whose names are hereto subscribed do by this agreement associate ourselves with the intention to constitute a corporation according to the provisions of the two hundred and seventeenth chapter of the General Court of the Commonwealth of Massachusetts formed in the year 1872 approved April 17th in said year, and the acts in amendment thereof.

The name by which the corporation shall be known is the,

==Franklin Library Association==

The purpose for which the corporation is constituted is to maintain a public library in the town of Franklin, and Reading Rooms in connection with the same. The town within which the corporation is established or located is the town of Franklin within said Commonwealth.

The said corporation may hold real and personal Estate necessary for the purposes of its organization to the amount of Fifty Thousand dollars, exclusive of Books, papers, collections in natural history and works of art.

In witness whereof we have hereunto set our hands this second day of September A.D. 1872.

Henry M. Greene
Francis B. Ray
Alphonse A. Russegue
Albert E. Daniels
James M. Freeman
Davis Thayer Jr.
Erastus E. Baker
Joseph G. Ray

The foregoing is a true copy of the agreement and names of the original members of the Corporation.

Attest A.A. Russegue, Clerk

Members of the Franklin Library Association

We the undersigned having been duly Elected members of the Franklin Library association in accordance with article Eleven of the By Laws thereof do hereby subscribe our names to the foregoing article of association.

Names of Corporators on Preceding Page-who are also members
J.A. Woodward
G.H. Morse
George W. Wiggin
Monroe Morse
Gardner Adams
George King
J.H. Wadsworth
H. A. Wyckoff
Wm. M. Thayer
A. H. Morse
Wm. E. Whiting
Salmon W. Squire

Waldo Daniels
A. Stanley
Wm. Rockwood
Adin D. Sargeant
Wm. B. Nolen
E.H. Sherman
L.W. Daniels
Jan. Mkmail—out of town, res. unknown
Henry W. Gay
A. {UNKNOWN NAME} Chambré—out of town; Lowell
Moses Darwin
Erastus L. Metcalf
A. G. Metcalf
George W. Ryan—out of town
Charles A. Grazer—out of town
John N. Short—out of town
Mrs. J. Ray—dead
Henry R. Jenks—dead
Henry C. Crane—out of town
James P. Ray—dead
Joseph Smith—dead
L.J. Fletcher—dead
A. L. Clark—resigned
Dwight M. Hodge—deceased
Lydia P. Ray—dead
H.R. Burringont—drafted 1914
Mary A. Wiggins—dead
Francis E. King—dead
Jenna N. Harrington—moved
Edward Neilly—dead
R.M. Farraim—deceased
Ella G. Campbell—deceased
Wm. H. Corby—resigned
Ernest D. Daniels—drafted 1914
Nathan C. Rye—dead
J.B. Woodland--?
Margaret L. Ray—resigned-dead
Charles J. M. Krangis—deceased
Carl B. Johnson—deceased
Adelbert D. Thayer--deceased
Annie Ray Thayer
Albert H. Martin
Orestes T. Doe

Mary E. Adams
Arthur W. Peirce
Robert W. Thayer
Nelson E. Newell
W.W. Dana
Irving H. Ganewell—dropped
Mary F. Johnson—moved
R. R. Wawa—moved
John Reid—moved
Rebecca Dunning—moved
Mrs. Cora Gina Daniels—dead
Clara E. Martin
Albert C. Monson
Alice Wiggin
Mabre P. Doe
Mary Farmming
Jennie P. Baker
William S. Richardson
Maud Stott

3/2/[19]15

Leroy W. Stott
Annie J. Stott--moved
Olive W. Nye
Lillian C. Hauer
Janette W. Martin
Ulysses L. Brunas
Arthur W. Hale—moved
Lucy E. Tower
Charles A.R. Ray
Frances Duke Ray Jan. 11-1923—moved
Marilyn R. Daniels
Helen A. Sinuardo
Mabel M. Mason
Bradley M. Rockwood
Alice J. Rockwood
Gertrude E. Thayer
{UNCERTAIN NAME}
Mrs. Chas. H. Motman
Jennie H. Abbott
Lee C. Abbott
Eva B. Laurence
Ezekiel M. Crowell--moved

Prince S. Crowell—moved
Marton Sanborn
Patty Sanborn
Albert F. Pally
M. Grace Brunas
Francis Patty
Oliver L. Hale
William S. Johnson
Kenneth P. Doe
Annie M. Woodward
Palmer A. Woodward
Gladys E. Mackenzie
Harlan R. Mackenzie
Susie M. Rick--moved
Gilbert W. Rick—moved
Earls M. Hand—moved
Lila W. Doe
Hope Lincoln—moved
Marion A. Ralston—moved
Albert P. Ralston—moved
Charles A. Richmond—moved
Mildred H. Richmond—moved
Charles F. Thayer
Mr. & Mrs. Harry J. Webb
Mr. & Mrs. Luther Buchanan
Mr. & Mrs. D. M. Angell—moved
Edna A. Bright
John R. Goodwin—3/3/36
Anna Pond Crowley 4-23-36
Walter F. Crowley M.D. 4-23-36
Lilian S. Roth 4-23-36
Leodre R. Roth 4-23-36
Helen H. Geeley—moved—4-23-36
Dr. J. Henry Geelery 4-23-36
Alauder C. Emen—moved
Florence L. Carmen—moved—4-23-36
Robert Cowen—moved—4-23-36
Dorothy W. Doe—moved—4-23-36
Edna T. Erren—moved
Donald B. Doe—moved
Albert E. Donald—moved
Helen A. Hutchinson—moved—1-23-39
Charles B. Hutchinson—moved—1-23-39

Rev. Mrs. Trueman J. Menadue—1-11-40
Donald B. Chapenace—moved
May Holmes 1-9-42
Florence V. U. Lincon 1-12-42
Ray E. Parmenter 1-13-42
Howard A. Lincoln 2-24-42
Edna W. Corr 2-24-42
Mary E. Kingsley 1-13-42
Waldo B. Arnold 2-10-44
Gertrude C. Glover 3-22-46
Frederick H. Glover 3-22-46 (deceased)
Ruth A. Kelly 6-8-47
Edith H. Garner 2-3-47
Mr. & Mrs. James H. Mulkeron 9-23-47
Mr. & Mrs. Barnard Backus 1/9/48 (Mrs. Deceased)
Mr. & Mrs. Ralph Howard 1/9/48
Mr. & Mrs. Peter Pasquantino 1/14/48
Richard F. Stack—Jan. 20, '48 (dead)
Marion E. Holmes 2/7/48
Dr. & Mrs. James Howard 9/30/48
Edmund J. Keefe 9/25/50
Mr. & Mrs. George P. Bentley 2/15/52
Mr. & Mrs. Howard C. Abbott 3/26/52
Elizabeth C. Brunelli 3/28/52
Clare L. Keefe 4/25/56
Clara M. Lodi 4/25/56
Eva L. Dana 4/25/56
Mr. & Mrs. Harmon W. Smith 4/25/56
Richard C. Howland 4/29/58
Beatrice F. Stack 4/29/58
Elizabeth R. Parmenter 4/29/58
Ruston F. Lodi 4/29/58

Annual Meeting—April 29, 1959

Ray E. Parmenter
Marjorie B. Metcalf
Jean Miller
Dorothy S. Drakenice
Rev. & Mrs. David Handers
Marion E. Holmes
Richard F. Stack—deceased
William R. Feeley
Morton W. Donahue

Alice Wiggin—deceased
Eileen L. Costello
Davis M. Abbott
Trueman John Menadue—deceased
Frank E. Hobston, Jr.
Margaret Axtell Crane—deceased
Anna E. Roth
Edmund J. Keefe
Clare L. Keefe
John R. Goodson—deceased
Lilian S. Roth—decease
Theodore R. Roth—deceased
Ruston Lodi
Howard C. Abbott
Richard C. Howland
Brunelli
Garner

Annual Meeting—April 24, 1963

Thurlo A. Russell
Ruston Lodi
Alice Wiggins
Ray E. Parmenter
Elizabeth R. Parmenter
Mr. & Mrs. Howard C. Abbott
Grace S. Poellnitz
Eileen L. Costello
Hen. C. Beavis
Lillian E. Duvall
J. F. Freeman
John Dahlgrant
Beatrice F. Stack
Mary S. Vanston
Edmund J. Keefe
Eva L. Donna
Helen L. Carberry
Wm. F. Carberry
Richard C. howland
Trueman J. Menadue
William C. Gamer
Florence P. DaVia
Betty M. Swenson
Hazel M. Gay

Jean Miller

Annual Meeting April 29, 1964

Mary E. Holmes
Marion E. Holmes
Lehau S. Roth
Elizabeth C. Brunelli
Doris M. Abbott
Lillian E. Duvall
Bertha Backuer
Gillant O. Dempsey
Florence Markee
David Clough Lukeus
Eleanor Reed Lukeus
P.J. Menadell
Thomas D. Maury
Margaret M. Mulcahey
Raymond G. Adams
Edmund J. Keefe
Jared Keefe
Betty M. Swenson
Hazel M. Gay
Jean Miller

Annual Meeting—1965

Treuman J. Menadue
Jeanette Harding
Martha Allen
John J. Allen Jr.
Barbara H. Janet
Georgann McDonald
Hazel L. Caton
Blanche E. Mayor
Joseph T. Mogue
Ray E. Parmenter
Helen Carberry
William F. Carberry

Betty M. Swenson
Carfoul C. Abbott
Paris M. Abbott
Leonard L. F. Remington
Elizabeth R. Parmenter
Grace S. Poeelmit
Eileen L. Costello
William H. Bonney
Dorothy J. Bonney
John Dahlgrun
Daniel McRowe
Mrs. Thomas P. Murray
Anne W. Rowe
Mrs. Rachael T. Stack
Gertrude Saven
Stella K. Jeon
Edmund J. Keefe

Annual Meeting—April 27, 1966

Mrs. Dorothy J. Bonney
Mr. & Mrs. William J. Merker
William H. Bonney
Hazel M. Gay
Francis Hunchard
Stella K. Jeon
Jeanette M. Harding
Clare S. Howard
Betty M. Swenson
Francis W. Webb
Elizabeth C. Brunelli
Clare Keefe
Edmund J. Keefe
Carlo B. Geromini
Mary E. Holmes
Marion E. Holmes
Margaret M. Murray
Stephanie S. Sullivan
Charles W. Desaulniers
Forter L. Cahoon
Franklin S. Crowther
Elizabeth F. Desaulniers
Lillian E. Duvall
Dorothy W. Arnet

Annual Meeting—April 25, 1967

William H. Bonney
Dorothy J. Bonney
Matthew Donahue
Joyce C. Adams
Hazel M. Gay
Francis Hunchard
Jean A. Hancock
Jean Miller
Jeanette Harding
Anna E. Roth
Margaret Axtall Crane
Martha M. Allen
John J. Allen, Jr.
Mrs. Richard T. Stock
Elizabeth Brunelli
Elizabeth R. Parmenter
Charles W. Desaulniers
Rev. & Mrs. Thomas Howard
Marion Holmes
Wm. F. Cailey
Lillian S. Roth
Lillian E. Duvall
Carlo B. Geromini
Eileen L. Costello
Clare Keefe
Doris M. Abbott
Thomas B. Murray
Mary E. Holmes
Francis W. Webb
Margaret M. Murray

Annual Meeting April 25, 1968

Janet M. Gaudrey
Frances W. Webb
Marion E. Holmes
Jeanette M. Harding
Doris M. Abott
Clare S. Howard

Dorothy J. Bonney
Edmund J. Keefe
Marty W. Donahue
Jean A. Hancock
Margaret M. Murray
Thomas P. Murray
Wm. F. Colby
Elizabeth T. Desaulniers
Charles W. Desaulniers
Carlo B. Geromini
Clare Keefe
Franklin S. Crowther
Eileen L. Costello
Betty M. Swenson
Stella K. Jeon

New Members

Sep. 30, 1968—John J. Brunelli
Anna G. Brunelli
Oct. 14, 1968—Yvonne W. Wahlers
Oct. 14, 1968—Edward John Jernip
Oct. 19, 1968—Mr. & Mrs. Robert Warber
Oct. 19, 1968—Barbara A. Levins
Oct. 22, 1968—Mr. & Mrs. Robert D. Costello
Nov. 12, 1968—Mr. & Mrs. Daniel J. Shanahan
Nov. 15, 1968—Mr. & Mrs. Robert J. Heming
Nov. 30, 1968—Alfred H. Wahler
Jun. 14, 1969—Elizabeth Eagles
Jun. 16, 1969—Mr. & Mrs. John Benpotts-moved to Wellesley
Jun. 25, 1969—Mr. & Mrs. James C. Hay
Jun. 30, 1969—Dergrine C. Hobbs
Jul. 7, 1969—Albert R. Brunelli
Oct. 15, 1969—Mr. & Mrs. Parker Vetrano
Oct. 24, 1969—Dr. & Mrs. William F. Brady Jr.
Oct. 24, 1969—Atty. & Mrs. Neil J. Rachel
4/15/70—Mr. & Mrs. N. B. Grime
4/15/70—Mr. & Mrs. S.E. Whitman
4/25/70 –Jerry W. Strok
4/26/70—Donna H. Strok

Annual Meeting April 29, 1969

Thomas P. Murray
Richard P. Carins

Charles W. Desaulniers
Betty M. Swenson
Margaret M. Murrary
Jeanette M. Harding
Hazel Gay
E. Jean Miller
Barbara Levine
John Levins
Clare Keefe
Ray E. Parmenter
Elizabeth R. Parmenter
Howard C. Abbott
Marion E. Holmes
John J. Brunelli
Eileen S. Costello
Eva L. Dana
Jean N. Hancock
Leonard L. Remington
Edward J. Keefe
Doris M. Abbott
Carlo B. Geromini
Janet M. Gaudrey
Betty M. Swenson

Annual Meeting, April 28, 1970

Grace A. Poellnitz
Jeanette M. Harding
Henry W. Strok
John E. Fitzgerald
Marvin E. Holmes
Barbara Levins
Jack Levins
William Brady
Helen J. Vetrano
Jean Costello
Clare Keefe
Dorothy Bonney
Eva L. Dana
Howard C. & Doris M. Abbott
Ray E. Parmenter
Jean H. Hancock
Eloise M. Hay
Carlo B. Geromini

John J. Brunelli Jr.
Francis W. Webb
Veronica C. Hobbs
John Beaufitts
Christie W. Hobbs
Richard P. Carins
Edmund J. Keefe
James C. Gay
A. Olsen
Betty M. Swenson
Kenneth A. Wood
Fuller R. Stevens
Eloise E. Pasquantino
Mary N. Hoyt—deceased
Helen L. Wood
Charles W. Desaulniers

New Members

Melvin J. Root
Alice C. Root
Frank A. Roach
Janet D. Roach

Annual Meeting, April 28, 1971

Grace S. Poellnitz
Helen J. Vetrano
Frederick R. Stearns Jr.
Barbara Levins
Jack Levins
Dorothy W. Abbott
Hazel M. Gay
John E. Fitzgerald
Dorothy J. Bonney
William H. Bonney
Melvin J. Root
Alice C. Root
Janet D. Roach
G.A. Hancock
Edwin E. Pasquantino
Edmund J. Keefe
Clare L. Keefe
Marin E. Holmes
Carlo B. Geromini

Doris M. Abbott
Veronica C. Hobbs
John Parker Velu
Mary E. Holmes
Albert W. Hobbs
A. E. Olsen
Marlene Baker
Daniel L. Baker
John Minot
E. Jean Miller
Mary D. McCahill
John Jane Cahill
Betty M. Swenson
Barbara Vipraio

New Members, '72

Barbara Vipraio
Julie Brennan (Mrs.)
John Brennan
Edwin F. Robert
Manuel Oordeci
Juliet M. Cordeu
Mr. & Mrs. Robert Brunelli
Mr. & Mrs. Robert Dunn

Annual Meeting, April 26, 1972

Annual Meeting
September 22, 1992

Henry J. Freniere
Linda M. Koplin
Barbara Vipraio
Maryjane M. Whiton
Pete B. Mulliken
Mary C. Chute
Howard J. Warrup
Mary Anne Squillace
Dorothy J. Bonney
Anne L. Whelan
Robert R. Keith

Annual Meeting
September 13, 1993

Barbara Vipraio
Elizabeth F. Waju
Dorothy Bonney
E. Jean Miller
Linda M. Koplin
Peter B. Mulliken
Robert A. Brown
Howard Warrup
Alice Vendetti
Clare M. Lodi
Barbara M. Smith
Helen J. Vetrano (Jackie)
Henry F. Freniere
Mary L. Chute
Anne L. Whelan
Mary Anne Squillace

Annual Meeting
September 27, 1994

Howard Warrup
Anne L. Whelan
Dorothy Bonney
Barbara M. Smith
Barbara L. Vipraio
Henry F. Freniere
Linda Koplin
Ed Padden
Mary Jane Whiton
Mary L. Chute
Mary Anne Squillace

Annual Meeting
September 26, 1995

Helen J. Vetrano (Jackie)
Linda Koplin
Henry F. Freniere
Mary L. Chute
Barbara Vipraio
Edward M. Padden
Richard L Whelan
Maryjane Gilleo-Whiton
Becky Terris
William H. Bonney

Clara M. Lodi
Anne L. Whelan

Annual Meeting
September 30, 1996

Anne L. Whelan
Peter B. Mulliken
Robert S. Brown
Barbara M. Smith
Becky Terris
Edward M. Padden
Clara M. Lodi
Richard L. Whelan
Henry F. Freniere

Annual Meeting
September 18, 1997

Anne L. Whelan
Bob Vipraio
Lori A. Herbert
Scott Hubert
Clara Lodi
Edward M. Padden
Robert S. Brown
Howard J. Warrup
Peter B. Mulliken
Barbara M. Smith
Mary E. Terris
Henry F. Freniere
Mary Anne Aquillan

Annual Meeting
January 12, 2005

Anne L. Whelan
Herbert L. Hunter
Peter B. Mulliken
Maryjane F. Whiton
Henry F. Freniere
Edward M. Padden
Vicki Buchanio
Elynor Crothers
Kent H. Wilder
Robert A. Brown
Christine L. Cabral

Annual Meeting
September 14, 2005

Anne L. Whelan
Henry F. Freniere
Robert S. Brown
Kent H. Wilder
Maryjane Whiton
Armand Fernandez
Felicia Oti
Clara M. Lodi
Barbara M. Smith
Vicki Buchanio
Elynor C. Crothers
Edward M. Padden

Annual Meeting
September 20, 2006

Nancy Canboy
Clara Lodi
Maryjane Whiton
Felicia Oti
Edward M. Padden
Vicki Buchanio
Glynor Crothers
Anne L. Whelan
Scott F. Nolan
Armand Fernandez

Annual Meeting
September 18, 2007

Felicia Oti
David C. Dahl
Vicki Buchanio
Clara Lodi
Maryjane Whiton
Armand Fernandez
Edward M. Padden
Elynor Crothers
Scott F. Nolan

**Meetings were held from 2008 thru 2012. The FLA Register for meeting attendance was unavailable to its members at this time. Meeting and minutes were kept as part of the record.*

Meet-May 13, 2013

Maryjane Whiton
Shirley Borusso
Celeste Johnson
Edward M. Padden
Elynor Crothers
Beth Mucciarone
Gregory Delluco
Scott F. Nolan
Armand Fernandez

Annual Meeting—October 23, 2013

Celeste Johnson
Maryjane Whiton
Joan McGuire
Armand Fernandez
Shirley Borruso
Edward M. Padden
Greg Dellorco
Scott F. Nolan, President

Annual Meeting-September 30, 2014

Beth A. Mucciarone
Jean McGuire
Maryjane Whiton
Scott F. Nolan, President
Edward M. Jackson
Nancy J. Rappa
Armand Fernandez
Celeste Johnson
Greg Dellorco
Shirley Borruso
Katie Kosek (FoFL)
Maria Lucier (FoFL)
Marjorie B. Dagle

Allen R. Earls
Monica B. Doyle
Sandi Brandfondbrenner
Barbara Andrews
Felicia Oti

Regular Meeting-November 12, 2014

Scott F. Nolan, President
Armand Fernandez, Treasurer
Shirley Borruso
Maryjane Whiton
Beth L. Mucciarone
Greg Dellorco
Edward Padden
Nany Rappa
Celeste Johnson

Note: The Franklin Library Association discussed the proposal submitted by Alan R. Earls and his son Eamon McCarthy Earls to produce a commemorative book of the history of the FLA. The content of the book will encompass the history of the town, the library and association. The response of the board was unanimous in moving forward to create the book. This is a milestone in the aggregation of history dating back to its inception October 2,1872 to today at 142 years old. It's remarkable the organization has sustained itself through its instruments ands and services remembering to stay the course in serving the inhabitants of Franklin.

Scott F. Nolan
President

Regular Meeting-May 20, 2015

Scott L. Nolan, President
Armand Fernandez—TREASURER
Edward Padden
Greg Dellorco
Beth A. Mucciarone
Shirley Borruso
Nancy J. Rappa

Annual Meeting, October 28, 2015

Scott F. Nolan, President
Nancy Rappa
Edward Padden
Beth A. Mucciarone
Greg Dellorco

Celeste Johnson
Maryjane Whiton
Armand Fernandez
Shirley Borruso

Regular Meeting, March 16, 2016

Scott F. Nolan, President
Judith Pond Piffer
Maryjane Whiton
Alan R. Earls
Edward M Padden
Nancy J. Rappa
Beth A. Mucciarone
Celeste Johnson
Shirley Borruso
Greg Dellorco
Joan McGuire
Felicia Oti

Regular Meeting, June 15, 2016

Scott F. Nolan, President
Nancy J. Rappa
Edward M. Padden
Greg Dellorco
Armand Fernandez-TREASURER
Shirley Borruso
Marjane Whiton

Note: The Board of Directors voted unanimously to annuitize its investments over a seven year period to July 2022. The decision was based on having the necessary funds available to preserve the historical books and documents that are part of the town's history. Discussion and support of the members present acknowledged the Franklin Library Association will close the chapter in its long history. It is the intent of this board to celebrate the Franklin Library's Association's 150th year anniversary with respect to its original founders and all that carried forth its mission to serve the inhabitants of Franklin. The renovations of the Ray Memorial Library and the new addition will continue to offer a place to read, study and embrace the technologies of the 21st century. The genealogy room will be named in the honor of the Franklin Library Association to serve as a place to honor and learn from the past. So be the thoughtful, planned, and honorable farewell to the FLA.

Scott F. Nolan
President
June 15, 2016
10:15pm

Annual Meeting, October 19, 2016

Scott F. Nolan, President
Judith Pond Pfeiffer, Construction Chair
Joseph A. Mullen
Nancy J. Rappa
Beth A Mucciarone
Armand Fernandez
Edward M. Padden
Maryjane Whiton
Greg Dellorco

Regular Meeting, July 12, 2017

Scott F. Nolan, President
Armand Fernandez – TREASURER
Maryjane Whiton
Joan McGuire
Beth A. Mucciarone
Edward M. Padden
Nancy J. Rappa

Annual Meeting, October 25, 2017

Judith Pond Pfeiffer
Nancy J. Rappa
Edward M. Padden
Beth A Mucciarone
Scott F. Nolan -President
Greg Dellorco
Shirley Borruso
Maryjane Whiton
Joan McGuire

Regular Meeting, January 10, 2018

Scott F. Nolan, President
Maryjane Whiton
Armand Fernandez – TREASURER
Nancy J. Rappa
Beth A. Mucciarone
Shirley J. Borusso

Regular Meeting, February 22, 2018

Scott F. Nolan, President
Armand Fernandez, -TREASURER

Edward M. Padden-Secretary
Greg Dellorco
Beth A. Mucciarone
Shirley Borruso
Maryjane Whiton
Nancy J. Rapa

The Board met with Alan Earls, author of the upcoming book on the history of the Franklin Library Association. All members were in attendance at the Nolan-Carlson home in Franklin. A lively conversation ensued on the history of the Ray Family, the trials, and tribulations of the FLA and how the current board members recall how each of us was recruited to serve. The board unanimously approved a handcrafted podium to be built-carved from wood to tell the story of the nation's first public lending library.

Scott F. Nolan
President

Regular Meeting, April 18, 2018

Scott F. Nolan, President
Beth A. Mucciarone
Edward M. Padden
Nancy J. Rappa
Armand Fernandez -TREASURER
Maryjane Whiton
Alan R. Earls guest

Annual Meeting, September 26,2018

Scott F. Nolan, President FLA
Armand Fernandez -TREASURER
Edward M. Padden -Secretary
Beth A Mucciarone
Joan McGuire
Maryjane Whiton
Nancy J. Rappa
Greg Dellorco

Regular Meeting, March 13, 2019

Armand Fernandez -TREASURER
Edward M. Padden -Secretary
Scott F. Nolan-President
Joan McGuire
Beth A. Mucciarone
Alan R. Earls
Maryjane Whiton

Greg Dellorco
Nancy J. Rappa
Shirley Borruso

Regular Meeting, May 1, 2019

Scott F. Nolan, President
Nancy J. Rappa
Beth A. Mucciarone
Joan McGuire
Edward M. Padden
Maryjane Whiton
Greg Dellorco

Annual Meeting, October 29. 2019

Scott F. Nolan, President
Armand Fernandez-TREASURER
Maryjane Whiton
Joan McGuire
Edward Padden
Beth A. Mucciarone
Greg Dellorco

BOARD MEETING -Feb. 19, 2020

Armand Fernandez – TREASURER
Scott F. Nolan – President
Edward M. Padden – Secretary
Nancy J. Rappa
Maryjane Whiton
Greg Dellorco
Beth Mucciarone
Shirley Borruso
Rocco Cavallaro
Vicki Buchanio Earls

Virtual Board Meeting – April 15, 2020
Scott F. Nolan, President
Armand Fernandez, Treasurer
Edward M. Padden, Secretary
Nancy J. Rappa
Beth Mucciarone
Gregg Delloroco
Shirley Borruso
Joan McGuire
Maryjane Whiton (Proxy)

Virtual Board Meeting – December 2, 2020
Scott F. Nolan, President
Armand Fernandez, Treasurer
Edward M. Padden, Secretary
Nancy J. Rappa
Beth Mucciarone
Gregg Delloroco
Shirley Borruso
Maryjane Whiton

FRANKLIN PUBLIC LIBRARY
118 Main Street
Franklin, Massachusetts 02038
Tel. 508-520-4940
http://town.franklin.ma.us

Felicia Oti
Director

Scott F. Nolan
President, Franklin Library Association
430 Franklin Village Drive, PMB# 300
Franklin, MA 02038

December 14, 2020

Dear Scott,

We are delighted with FLA's decision to fund the Library's request for $46,624 to digitize the Town of Franklin's List of Residents. We are particularly grateful because we know that digitizing our historical collections would preserve and provide the community with easy access to this information.

Thank you for your continued support and commitment to funding future preservation projects.

Sincerely,

Felicia Oti
Library Director

Virtual Board Meeting – January 13, 2021

Scott F. Nolan, President
Armand Fernandez, Treasurer
Edward M. Padden, Secretary
Nancy J. Rappa
Beth Mucciarone
Shirley Borruso
Maryjane Whiton

Franklin Library Association
Virtual Meeting

Wednesday, October 6, 2021

Members present: Scott Nolan, Edward Padden, Armand Fernandez, Beth Mucciarone, Nancy Rappa, Maryjane Whiton (proxy)

President Nolan opened the meeting at 6:10 p.m.

1. Armand report – present amount $103,073.26 with one more payment for August, 2022 of $54,000 – total $157,023.26.

Future bills – 1) 2021 IRS, 2) 2022 IRS, 3) final financial report for disband – Armand estimates these costs at $85,00 – suggests we only commit $56,000 for 2021 – allocate $75,000 and hold $21,000

2. Review of Vicki's list – (Rockwood etc.)

3. Review of Memorial Hall, Delivery Room, Reading Gallery Room

4. VOTED : $20,500 for manuscripts and $45,000 for Delivery Room = $65,000 (upper +10)

5. Rocco? Alan Earls? Scott will check

6. Adjournment – 7:10 p.m.

Respectfully Submitted,

Edward Padden, Secretary

FRANKLIN PUBLIC LIBRARY
America's First Public Library
118 Main Street
Franklin, Massachusetts 02038-1992
Tel. (508) 520-4940

Scott F. Nolan
President, Franklin Library Association
430 Franklin Village Drive, PMB# 300
Franklin, MA 02038

December 30, 2021

Dear Scott,

We are delighted with the Franklin Library Association's unanimous decision to provide $65,500 for the restoration of the murals in *the* Delivery Room and the preservation of seven Historical Manuscripts.

Your generous donation will make it possible for the Library to take the first critical steps in restoring this unique masterpiece to its original splendor, and in ensuring that generations to come will value and cherish it.

Thank you on behalf of the staff and the citizens of the town of Franklin.

Sincerely,

Felicia Oti

Felicia Oti
Library Director

Franklin Library Association

Annual Meeting

November 15, 2022

The Annual Meeting of the Franklin Library Association was held on Tuesday, November 15, 2022 at the Franklin Public Library, 118 Main Street, Franklin, Massachusetts.

Members present: Scott Nolan, Armand Fernandez, Edward Padden, Nancy Rappa, Beth Mucciarone, Joan McGuire, Shirley Borruso, and Gregory Dellorco.

Invitee Present: Alan Earls

President Nolan opened the meeting at 6:00 p.m.

1. Armand submitted his latest Treasurer's Report (see attached copy). The report indicated a checking account balance as of November 15, 2022 of $84,680.74 with a grand total of expected withdrawals of $83,550,00 with an expected balance of $1,230.74 as of December 31, 2022. These figures of expenses and balances are estimates as of November 15, 202. Armand stressed the importance of spending the monies prior to December 31, 2022 leaving only a small balance for final expenses.

2. Armand proudly stated that the FLA has spent approximately $522,000 in recent years on library preservation and other related expenses.

3. Armand then explained the line-by-line figures on the Treasurer's Report.

4. The more monies that the FLA expends by December 31, 2022, the easier will be the final accounting in early 2023.

5. Reference is made to a letter from Vicki Earls to the John Canning Company in regard to a priority list for the expenditure of remaining FLA funds. See attached

6. Scott reported that Canning has agreed to perform the work in Vicki's letter for the lower figure of $65,000.

7. A motion was made and seconded and was unanimously

VOTED: to expend $65,000 to the John Canning Company to perform the work described in Section 1 of Vicki's proposal

8. A motion was made and seconded and was unanimously

VOTED: to expend the sum of $5,000 for Vicki's latest proposal headed Manuscripts. See attached

9. Alan Earls reported that the long-awaited book is just about ready and discussed the possible different styles such as regular paperback, cloth cover or leather cover. After discussion a motion was made and seconded and unanimously

VOTED: to purchase 100 copies of the proposed book at $13.00 per copy and 15 copies of the special leather-bound book at $175 per copy for a total cost of $3,925. These figures are estimates but close to Armand's projected figures in the Treasurer's Report.

10. A motion was made and seconded and was unanimously

VOTED: to place the balance of funds remaining after the above expenditure and other incidentals in escrow in the name of Christopher Feeley, Agent, such funds to distributed in early 2023 prior to dissolution. These funds shall be classified as "excess undistributed funds" and shall total not less than $2,500.

There being no further business, President Nolan adjourned the meeting at 7:10 p.m.

Town of Franklin

355 East Central Street
Franklin, Massachusetts 02038-1352

Phone: (508) 520-4949
www.franklinma.gov

Office of the Town Administrator

Memorandum

December 9, 2022

To: Town Council

From: Jamie Hellen, Town Administrator
Alecia Alleyne, Assistant to the Town Administrator

Re: Resolution 22-86: Gift Acceptance - Franklin Public Library

---

The Franklin Public Library has received an exceptionally generous donation in the amount of $70,000 from the Franklin Library Association. This donation will be allocated towards the cleaning and conservation of *Memorial Hall (entrance) "Hours of the Day"* Frieze by Tommaso Julgaris as proposed by John Canning & Company, as well as the digitization of the *Sanitary Survey of the Town of Franklin* and the *1875 Map of the Town of Franklin*.

This donation is especially meaningful as, after 150 years of operation, the Franklin Library Association will be closing its doors at the end of this year. On behalf of the Town of Franklin and the Franklin Public Library, we extend our deepest gratitude to the Franklin Library Association for many years and countless examples of their consistent and incredible support.

If you have any additional questions please feel free to ask.

Sponsor: Administration

TOWN OF FRANKLIN
RESOLUTION 22-86

Acceptance of Gift – Franklin Public Library

WHEREAS, The Franklin Public Library has received a generous donation totaling $70,000 to be allocated towards the cleaning and conservation of Memorial Hall (entrance) "Hours of the Day" Frieze by Tommaso Julgaris as proposed by John Canning & Company, as well as the digitization of the Sanitary Survey of the Town of Franklin and the 1875 Map of the Town of Franklin.

Donation Summary:

1. Franklin Library Association - $70,000.00

NOW THEREFORE, BE IT RESOLVED THAT:

The Town Council of the Town of Franklin on behalf of the Franklin Public Library gratefully accepts this generous donation to be used at the discretion of the Franklin Public Library as described above.

This resolution shall become effective according to the provisions of the Town of Franklin Home Rule Charter.

DATED: ____________, 2022

VOTED: ____________________________

UNANIMOUS: _______________

A TRUE RECORD ATTEST:

YES: _________ NO: _________

ABSTAIN:_____ ABSENT: _____

RECUSED: _________________

Nancy Danello, CMC
Town Clerk

____
Glenn Jones, Clerk
Franklin Town Council

Franklin Library Association

An investment in knowledge always pays the best interest.

November 27, 2021

Hello Felicia

The last annual meeting of the Franklin Library Association (FLA) was held on Wednesday, November 15th at the Franklin Library meeting room. Attached is a copy of the article written in the *Franklin Observer* published on November 16th, 2022. It was with excitement we held the last meeting to approve the following:

- The board unanimously approved the final proposal dated November 15th, 2022, for the scope of the work submitted to *John Canning & Company* as outlined for $65,000.00 (see attachment)
- The board unanimously approved $5000.00 for the digitization of the *Sanitary Survey of the Town of Franklin* and the *1875 Map of the Town of Franklin.*

We would like to present a check to you at the next Town Council Meeting in the amount of $70,000 with restrictions for the preservation, restoration, and digitization as appropriate to the item approved by the board of directors as listed above.

On behalf of the Franklin Library Association, it has been an honor and a privilege to serve this community in fulfilling the mission of the Ray Family and all the members over the past 150 years to preserve history, add custom historical pieces, and leave a legacy that tells the story of the founding of the FLA to present.

Our shared desire is that the town and greater community will continue to preserve, protect, and fund this historical treasure for the next 150 years!

With kind regards,

Scott F. Nolan

Scott F. Nolan
President FLA

Attachments:

Franklin Observer (11/16/2022) - After 150 Years, Library Association Holds Final Annual Meeting

John Canning & Co., Proposal (11/15/2022) – Restriction of $65,000 for scope of work as outlined

[NB. Date on letter should have been 2022]

Appendix B: An overview of the history of the Friends of the Franklin Library

At the time period that the library was transitioning from its tripartite origins — with the Ray Library Association owning the building, the Franklin Library Association providing much of the funding, and the town handling day-to-day operations -- a group of citizens saw a need for a new organization — a "friends" group that could engage the public in supporting the library politically and financially.

To that end, in July of 1982 a group met with a representative of the Friends of the Bellingham Library to get ideas on starting a Franklin friends group to benefit the Franklin Library. The meeting, led by Vilma Pascucci, included Barbara Rondeau, Angela Nasuti, Alice Beane, and Florence Chisholm.

Clearly that first meeting bore fruit because within two years a full-fledge organization, the Friends of the Franklin Library (FOFL), was operating in town. A typed Friends meeting minutes from August of 1984 lists Vilma Pascucci as president, Florence Chisholm Treasurer along with members such as `Angie' Nasuti, Madeline and Joseph Nasuti, Cathy Mucciarone, Daniele Dannelle, Marion Cleeton, John Ristaino, and Liz Brunelli. At that point, ambitious plans were afoot for the celebration of the 80th anniversay of the Ray building and to mark the transfer of ownership to the town.

Showcasing an early readiness to act and to put money behind their sentiments, the meeting saw passage of a motion by Marion Cleeton to donate $200 toward restoration of the portraits of Rev. Emmons, a key figure in the town and the early history of the library, as well as purchasing 70 magazine storage boxes.

And the group was attracting plenty of individuals willing to put time into the organizations. The August meeting, held at the library, saw Barbara Jarrett elected as the new president with Roger Rondeau taking on the duties of vice president. Marion Cleeton and Cathy Mucciarone filled out the slate as treasurer, and recording secretary respectively. Only a month later, the Friends were busy with a "very successful" book fair held on the library grounds; one of scores conducted over the subsequent years.

The changing of the guard "ceremony," which the Friends helped orchestrate, occurred in early October with recognition to the Ray Memorial Library Association, under whose guidance the building had been maintained for eight decades, The Franklin Library Association, under whose jurisdiction the library was operated, and the town, which paid for the operation of the library within the building.

According to an article at the time titled "Spotlight to Shine on Ray Building" from the *Woonsocket Call* newspaper, "The accompanying exhibits were planned to trace the history of the library including its lengthy closure in 1981" because of the concerns about the structural integrity of the roof and its subsequent repair. Also to be acknowledged in the reopening of the library was the major effort of the Franklin Historical Commission and the town to "save the library" including the not inconsiderable "red tape" involved in having the Ray Memorial Association turn the building over to the town...and the town's subsequent formal takeover of full operational responsibility for the library.

Not the least of the treats planned was a visit from the niece of Lydia Ray Peirce and Annie Ray Thayer — Charlotte Ray — who had maintained an interest and involvement in her family's largesse over the decades.

The speakers the friends included numbered among them Henry L. Freniere, chairman of the Franklin Library Advisory Board; town council chairman Daniel J. Gilmore, Massachusetts Senator Ed Brooke, Gilbert O. Dempsey, past president of the Franklin Library Association, and Vilma G. Pascucci, founder of the Friends of the Franklin Library.

Of course, the library continued to spark support from others in the community with a long history of involvement. On Jan, 22, 1985, the newspaper reported that the Aldenettes, a division of the Alden Club, had volunteered their members' time to update library card records and prepare cards for mailing. Volunteers on the project included Lillian Duvall, Margie Gilmore, Pattie Kavanaugh, Jayne Kittredge, Janet Norman, and Patrica Ober.

The major library renovations that followed in the late 1980s, gutted much of the original structure and removed much loved architectural details. It also seemed to have put a dent the activities of the Friends judging by the paucity of records for the period. However, the leadership and rank-and-file members came roaring back when the beautifully enlarged facility reopened in 1989.

It was a time to celebrate but also a time to come to the defense of the library. A national recession, felt most severely in Massachusetts, devastated state finances, threw thousands out of work, dented rising real estate values, and put local spending under threat.

December of 1990 saw library director Mary Chute's request for $72,549 to meet state accreditation guidelines turned down by the hard-pressed town finance committee – despite a room full of "concerned citizens" – including many FOFL members. But the show of support may have had an effect because just two days later the *Milford Daily News* reported gleefully that the "Franklin [Town] Council Saves Library" — voting 11-2 to provide a compromise figure of $33,350 in restored funding so that the library could remain open 40 hours a week rather than just 20. But the *Call* termed the victory, accurately, a half-a-loaf, which still compelled the library to cut its staff by 50 percent.

Finance Committee Vice Chair Judith Pfeffer was asked to explain the Finance Committee's 10-0 vote against providing additional funds, "The Finance Committee is in sympathy with the library, but is cognizant that other town departments, like fire and police, were also cut," she told the *Call*.

Now it was that the Friends entered upon the broad-shouldered task of helping to fill the funding shortfalls that appeared likely to persist for some time to come, by initiating more imaginative and frequent fund-raising activities.

Combining both entertainment, education, and fundraising the Friends invited internationally recognized antique doll experts, George and Florence Theriault, to provide a presentation and lecture at the library in June of 1991. With a modest appraisal fee of only $10, much of which went to fundraising, an enthusiastic crowd shared their beloved childhood keepsakes or acquired collectibles. One of the attendees was retired academic librarian and Franklin Library volunteer, Wilma Winter. Based on the appraisal she received, Winter opted to sell one of her treasured dolls on the spot and donated the proceeds — $140-— to the Friends. Memorializing the donation a few days later, Friends President Robert Brown wrote to thank Wilma and said, "we are grateful for your wonderful gesture." In total the event raised some $800.

In 1991, the Friends were also acknowledging a gift from Waldenbooks, a large national chain store, in support of the book sale.

As the organization's activities grew more extensive and complex, the need to update and expand FOFL bylaws also became clear. A new body of bylaws was approved on May 12, 1992. It opened with a section listing the organization's objectives:

1. To stimulate public interest, community awareness and support of the Franklin Library by interpreting, to the public, its services and needs;
2. To provide an orderly means for using specialized abilities and talents of the member of the corporation and its resources for the benefit of the Library;
3. To maintain a liaison with the Library Director and staff;
4. To provide financial support to meet such specialized library needs as may be approved by the Board of Directors of the Friends.

Meanwhile, long-time board member Marion Cleeton offered her resignation due to her commitment to teach night classes at Dean. And the May 2, 1995 annual meeting at the library, led by president Peter Mulliken, saw Bob Brown of the nominating committee propose Colin Cass, Wilma Winters and Nancy Conboy to fill vacant two-year terms on the board — a measure which quickly passed. Mary Chute used the meeting to acknowledge the work of the group and stress its continued importance in supplementing existing bare-bones library services.

Perhaps those words helped fortify the FOFL for its next triumph. As if book sales, cultural sponsorships, and regular efforts to assess the library's needs weren't enough to keep the organization busy, in 1995, the Friends hosted one of their most ambitious fund-raising efforts ever –one that is remembered fondly by those who participated. "Murder at the Franklin Library" — A murder mystery/audience participation play, was held on Oct 27 at the library by the Friends and featured wine, coffee, and desserts for a ticket price of $20.00. The "whodunit," with community members taking on a variety of roles, was a success financially and also boosted community participation in the library. And a lot of people left the library with smiles on their faces.

But less light-hearted activities also required time, commitment – and money – from the Friends. At the April 3, 1996 regular meeting Bob Brown update everyone on "the photocopier situation." At the time, even something as basic as a photocopier was not part of the town's library budget. So, Brown did his homework, laid out the options, and encouraged the board to purchase a used model for the library's use. This the board did; approving an expenditure of $1,800 to purchase the machine as well as an annual $375 maintenance contract.

Recognizing both the successes of the organization and its need to continue to engage the public for support, Bob also discussed plans for a "Friends Kiosk" to be placed in the library to display information about the organization and the library.

And, while the copier was badly needed and much appreciated, new library director Betsy Ferris came to the September meeting with another concern. Times were changing – fast. The Internet and World Wide Web were rapidly becoming indispensable for libraries and the public, with relatively few ways to "get online" was anxious to find a path to the online world through the library. The library itself was going online through the Minuteman Library Network and hoped to adopt a first wave of automation, for which support might be needed.

Meanwhile, of course, books and their care remained paramount. And the Friends again came to the rescue, providing $2,500 for an exterior book drop — designed to avoid the risk of fire presented by an indoor drop.

Where would the money come from? Book sales remained the Friend's staple activity. In fact, Anne M. Giordano reported in November of 1996 that the Fall book sale had raised more than $2,000.

During 1996 the Friends were also discussing updates to bylaws, for example changing the terms of the board, and setting term dates to encourage a regular addition of new people.

The year ended on a lively note with a successful gift-wrapping fundraiser event at Barnes and Noble in Bellingham that raised more than $200. It was money that would be sorely needed in the new year.

For example, Enid Gilbert provided a number of updates to the Friends on the English as a

Second Language (ESL) program that the Friends supported at the library as well as an introductory citizenship program for those interested in pursuing that path.

In the Spring, Susan McAlister (attending in place of Betty Ferris) reported that the library was looking into lending out CDs and software and that Vicki Buchanio was working to build the library's music CD collection. Meanwhile, Bob Brown reported on his attendance at a meeting of the Franklin Library Association. He said that the group was "reorganizing" and focusing narrowly on a few areas such as library preservation. In fact, he said, the FLA members had asked whether the Friends might take on more of the responsibilities traditionally handled by FLA.

At mid-year the treasurer reported a balance of $9208, a figure that included $2200 earned at the Spring book sale. Finally, a milestone was noted when Ken Norman recognized Wilma Winter for her years of dedication as she retired from FOFL. A book (subsequently discarded by the library in 2015) was donated to the library in her name.
With a well-oiled organization and ongoing budget shortfalls – as well as an ambitious list of proposed activities – the next several years fell into a pattern of book sales, gifts received, support for a wide range of library programs, and leadership shown in countless vital ways.

From Sept 1998 to June 1999 the Friends had planned a half-dozen programs for the library including Making Beer at Home, Preparing your Car for Winter, Winter Bird Feeding, and Landscaping. Plans were revealed for a Fall book sale to commemorate the 10th anniversary of the library renovation. In keeping with the professionalism of the group, the occasion was also being used to "study the book sale process" and ensure it was working as well as possible. Other projects included conversations with Tri-County Vocational-Technical High School about constructing the long-sought kiosk for the Friends at the library. And the Friends worked with Betsy Ferris to provide a "changing area" for infants in the library. Objections from the Board of Health needed to be answered, particularly the problem of trash at the library, which was only being emptied weekly. Keeping its commitment to the community, the Berner Family Trust made a donation of $1000 to the Friends.

Other topics swirling around the Friends included plans for a Jazz Night fundraiser, the possibility of purchasing an additional copier for the library, a possible cookbook fundraiser and an effort by Bob Brown and Anne Giordano to sell some of the more unique books on offer at the library book sale online at higher prices, and, finally, a Library Lovers Month celebration. An offer to pay for a new outdoor library sign was conveyed from the Rotary Club by member Paul Cheli with the stipulation that it include the Rotary Club logo.

To help manage and lead all these initiatives, as 2000 began, the Friends included five very busy subcommittees, namely:

* Membership
*Public relations/public education

*program
*Fundraising
* Nominating

New members were still coming into the Friends and Bob Brown reported 53 renewals in February alone — all of which helped to take the treasury to more than $9,000.

Supplementing the busy slate of activities surrounding the October book sale, the Friends also sponsored programs such as Dried Flower Topiaries, a performance by the Hopkinton Chamber Orchestra, How to Buy a Home Computer, and Genealogy talks.

2001 saw robust new member growth in February and in March and a request from the library director for a new CD rack to house the growing CD collection that the Friends had supported.

But in a growing town with constant need for fresh municipal spending, the library budget was ever in peril. June saw Ferris reporting that again "the budget looks bad." Modified staff hours and cuts in part time positions were a first consequence and, longer term, hopes to create a formal archive for the fragile and historically significant holdings had to be scrapped. By September, the situation was no better, but at last the long-needed library parking lot on the corner of School and Main Streets was under construction.

Individual in-memorium donations continued to arrive unbidden. Among those memorialized with multiple donations were Mary Woods, mother of long-time library employee Janice Roddy and Maybelle E. Remington Pond, mother of long-time town council member Judith Pond Pfeffer.

The cold winds of January 2002 brought no great improvement in the library's budget. Betsy Ferris asked that the Friends continue to sustain the literacy program since no money was available in the regular budget. Despite that sobering news, the Friends also prepared to help in celebrating the Ray Memorial Library's 100th anniversary in 2004. A list of areas needing "sprucing up" was begun, such as sections of the foyer and worn floor grates. Of equal importance was a visit by Interim Library Director Felicia Oti who asked the Friends to formally sponsor the planned centennial celebration. Fortuitously, the Friends could report a bank balance in excess of $21,000 as of June and plunged into plans for a Volunteer Fair to include the Friends' Literacy Link, Library Board of Directors, and Library Preservation Committee.

In January of 2004, Felicia Oti, formerly the Assistant Library Director, returned and reported that she had accepted a position as the new Director of Library Services. At that time, she requested funds for a previously discussed flatbed scanner and a digital camera. She also asked Peter Mulliken if he would approach the FLA to determine when money from that organization might be made available for preservation projects.

Shortly thereafter, in March, Oti approached the Friends and asked for $15,000 to purchase books. Bob Brown responded that the annual budget for the Friends stood at about $12,000 and that included support for a wide range of programs that the organization did not wish to abandon.

Director Oti attended the April meeting and proposed encouraging patrons to "adopt a book," donate to the library gift fund, or join the Friends. There was support for these ideas, but a request in September for a microwave oven and a refrigerator for the staff room was not approved. Members present suggested those purchases should come from the town budget.

Meanwhile, Mary Ann Squillace reported the original sketches for the reading room paintings were in the process of being restored with FLA funds. She expressed an interest in holding a fundraiser to acquire funds ($20,000-30,000) for repair of the the faux marble and other building restoration projects. She asked if the Friends would coordinate and offered to hold an art show at her residence with a $50 per person admission, with the artists contributing a portion of their sales.

The following years saw a continuation of the successful book sales and ongoing attempts to get the library director to prioritize her needs for consideration by the friends, with mixed results; leading to funding for some items and not others.

Incoming president Rebecca Cole Maselli welcomed the attendees to the board meeting in September of 2005 with a litany of planned programs including an Ice Cream Social, a Barber Shop Quartet, participation in the Downtown Partnership's Harvest Festival, Backyard Birds of Massachusetts, a talk by local author Michael Tougias, Parapsychology, Stage Magic, Emergency Preparedness, plans for Ben Franklin's 300th birthday, Library Lover's Month, and an Investment Panel.

The following month a key topic was the need to create an updated website for the Friends.

When the new year came around, the Friends were spearheading the January celebration of Franklin's birthday, including outreach to Dr. Robert Allison, a prominent Massachusetts historian, to provide a talk on the town's famous benefactor. On a lighter note, well-known Franklin impersonator Bill Merkle, and school groups would be performing as part of the celebration.

Early in the year, Library Director Oti shared plans with the Friends to close off the ceiling of the children's room to add more floor area in the adult section located on the floor above. She explained that the construction would start in April and inquired about her spending requests. The board, in turn, asked her to provide more specifics and a breakdown of costs.

Despite these delays and the growing back-and-forth between the Friends and the director, the treasurer was able to report that 80 percent of the group's funds had gone to the library over the previous year, with the balance covering expenses. And the goal remained reaching a level of 90 percent disbursements.

Toward that end Lesley McCaffrey proposed an ambitious fall fundraiser with either a jazz theme, at the Franklin Country Club, or with a country and western theme at the Cole Tavern.

A year later, in February of 2008, with $30,000 in its accounts, Bob Brown recommended that the Friends offer three spending options to the library director...and Lesley McCaffrey spoke in favor of simply buying books rather than just providing unencumbered cash.

But, not for the last time, the Friends – as advocates for the library – had a bigger challenge to worry about.

In May, Cole Maselli discussed plans for a rally in support of the library. Municipal finances were again in disarray and a May 22 override vote held the key. If it passed, the library would safe but if it failed, operating hours would have to be slashed from 62 to 36. The Friends agreed to spend for yard signs in support of the override – and the treasurer reported that the organization would likely carry $18,000 into the new fiscal year "depending on book sale profits."

Remarkably, the Friends could share some credit for helping to pass the Town's first-ever operational override for $2.7 million. But, of course, it wouldn't be the last library fiscal crisis.

The Friends had done much, both supporting the library politically and providing important extras. Summarizing the achievements, the Friends published a brochure showcasing their tremendous contribution over a seven-year period.

2011	16,726
2010	20,031
2009	17,039
2008	33,337
2007	31,634
2006	29,734
2005	20,454
Total	168,955

Again, the town finances left no room to fully fund library operations — and the Friends did their best to rally the town, but to no avail.

And relations between the Friends and the library director remained complicated. For instance, in June of 2013, the board received a request for $4,027.47 for the children's room but with no details. Oti later amended the request to explain its purpose and the board voted to approve the request.

It was noted that this was the only documented request for funds received during the calendar year to that point.

As the book sale had grown, the DPW had offered to make available its ample garage building on Hayward Street to accommodate a larger event. The DPW also made space available to store hundreds of boxes of books prior to the event.

An analysis of the event for the year showed that just counting volunteers (not board members), individuals logged more than 471 hours preparing for the event or running the event. And it wasn't just the town and the library that benefited. Inmates at the Norfolk Prison received 24 boxes of books remaining from the sale.

But success turned out to be a swan song: the library board of directors unexpectedly ruled that the Friends would no longer be *allowed* to hold a book sale to benefit the library. This came as a shock to those in attendance at the Sept. 4, 2013 meeting: Maria Lucier, Frank Nosek, Kevin O'Malley, Joe Mullen, Jan Martin, Barbara Christensen, Jim Beaulieu, Kathie Nosek, Carolyn Marr, Kit Wilcox, Phil Sweeney, and Vidya Iyer.

Lucier, spoke up in defense of the Friends book sale, which had brought in much more money than the ongoing library book sale, which Oti had initiated, occupying space outside her office and seemingly using staff time. Furthermore, Lucier noted that across the state and across the country, friend groups were invariably the entity to sponsor and run fundraising book sales. Lucier also pointed out that her research had shown that library administrators generally made time to attend meetings of friends groups. However, she noted, in the case of the Friends of the Franklin Library, Oti had attended only five of the previous 22 meetings and Monique Doyle, a member of the Library Board, 13 of the 22.

After a lengthy discussion about the disappointing development, it was decided to let all members know by email about the cancellation of the sale and to document all the frustrations the Friends had faced along with recommended solutions. And rather than letting the dispute make its way into the newspapers, potentially inflaming the already difficult situation, the group agreed to reach out to Town Administrator Jeffry Nutting.

In addition to the loss of revenue to the organization from cancelling the event, board members noted that others would be affected too, including the Franklin Food Pantry, teen volunteers, library volunteers, prisoners that had received access to books, teachers that had been given the chance to get free books for their classrooms, and the larger Franklin community.

To add insult to injury, at the request of the Library Board, a motion was made to turn over the entire net proceeds from the May book sales ($7160.52) to the Library Board, without any information provided to the Friends as to its use. This was defeated by a unanimous vote.

Things were no better in January of 2014 when Oti and Doyle suggested that the Friends simply issue a check for $10,000 to be used for any purpose by the library. The minutes noted that "This was met with hesitation from the Friends since the library director was not willing to submit an account of how the money will be used and which programs or passes were funded." Outreach to the town administrator proved fruitless.

March came in like a lion with Oti reminding the Friends that they would not be allowed to run any programs at the library, such as author talks, "due to union rules." She suggested they instead consider running off-site activities and acting as "ambassadors" to the Downtown Partnership in her stead. Finally, she told the Friends that suggestions from the public about library operations or acquisitions should be directed only to her, not the Friends.

Seeking a constructive path forward, the friends sought advice from Alice M. Welch of the Massachusetts Board of Library Commissioners regarding methods for ensuring good and effective relations between the Friends and the library board and director. Welch attended the April meeting and noted that since the organizations (the Friends, the Library Board, and the Town Library) are legally separate, written records would be important to maintain so as to document actions. She suggested creating a memorandum of understanding (MOU) to govern future relations in general.

In the meantime, Oti wrote to the Friends asking for a $10,000 donation to fund summer programs. This, the Friends took under consideration.

The year also saw the first awarding of a scholarship in honor of a career librarian and long-time active member, Wilma Winter. This was valued at $1000 and awarded to Marissa Palladini, from the Franklin High school class of 2014, one of about 40 students that applied.

In the winter of 2015, the Friends reported a second scholarship on offer, for an additional $1000 to students graduating from Tri-County Regional Vocational Technical High School.

And while relationships within the library community continued to simmer, plans bubbled up from town government to dramatically expand the library building – a project that they duly approved and funded. And that meant the library would soon have to relocate to temporary quarters while construction was underway.

Related to this effort, in May of 2016, the Friends voted to gift $25,000 to the library for digitizing and preserving items in the "quiet room" while they were being packed for the library's move.

Proposed digitizations ranged from 1814 handwritten arithmetic books, Ray Memorial Assocation hand-written minutes, hand written notes about marking the boundaries of

Franklin, Wrentham, and Bellingham, the *Franklin Register* newspaper, the vital records portions of Franklin town reports from 1858 and other similar historical records, some of which were held at the town museum.

In the years leading up to 2022, the Friends continued their robust and wide-ranging support of the library and related aspects of community service and, as the Franklin Library Association 'sunsets' will doubtless continue that shared tradition of activism and advocacy.

Appendix C: Books Donated by Benjamin Franklin*

Clark's Works,4 vols., folio
Hoadley's Works, 3 vols., folio
Barrow's Works, 2 vols., folio
Ridgley's Works, 2 vols., folio
Locke's Works, 1 vol., octavo
Sydney's Works, 1 vol., octavo
Priestley's Corruptions, 2 vols.
Price and Priestly, 1 vol.
Lyndsey's Apology and Sequel, 2 vols.
Abernathy's Sermons, 2 vols.
Duchal's Sermons, 3 vols.
Price's Morals, 1 vol.
Price on Providence, 1 vol.
Price on Liberty, 1 vol.
Price on the Christian Scheme, 1 vol.
Needham's Free State, 1 vol.
West and Littleton on the Resurrection, 1 vol.
Stenner's Sermons, 2 vols.
Addison's Evidences, 1 vol.
Gordon's Tacitus, 5 vols.
Bachus' History, 1 vol.
Lardner on the Logus, 1 vol., 8 vo.
Watt's Orthodoxy and Charity, 1 vol.
Brainerd's Live, 1 vol.
Bellamy's True Religion, 1 vol.
Dodderidgel's Life, 1 vol.
Bellamy's Permission of Sin, 1 vol.
Fordyce's Sermons, 1 vol.
Hemminway against Hopkins, 1 vol.
Hopkins on Holness, 1 vol
Fulfilling the Scriptures, 1 vol.
Montesquieu's Spirit of Laws, 2 vol.
Blackstone's Commentaries, 4 vols.

Watson's Tracts, 6 vols.
Newton on the Prophesies, 3 vols
Law on Religion, 1 vol.
Priestley's Institutes, 2 vols.
Watts on the Passions, 1 vol.,
Watt's Logic, 1 vol.
Edwards on Religion, 1 vol.
Dickinson on the Five Points, 1 vol.
Christian History, 2 vols.
Prideaux's Connections, 4 vols.
Cooper on Predestination, 1 vol.
Cambridge Platform, 1 vol.
Stoddard's Safety of Appearing, 1 vol.
Burkett on Personal Reformation, 1 vol.
Barnard's Sermons, 1 vol.
Sheppard's Sound Believer, 1 vol.
History of the Rebellion, 1 vol.
Janeway's Life, 1 vol.
Hopkins' System, 2 vols.
American Preacher, 4 vols.
Emmons Sermons, 1 vol. {Clearly not part of the original collection}
Thomas' Laws of Massachusetts, 1 vol.
American Constitutions, 1 vol.
Young's Night Thoughts, 1 vol.
Pilgrim's Progress, 1 vol.
Ames' Oration, 1 vol.
Spectators, 8 vols.
Life of Baron Trenk, 1 vol.
Cheap Repository, 2 vols.
Moral Repository, 1 vol.
Fitch's Poem, 1 vol.
Erskine's Sermons, 1 vol.
Life of Cromwell, 1 vol

** This listing is based on a 19th Century inventory and clearly includes some titles not from Franklin*

Index

U

V

W

References

[i] Franklin Library Association - A Tribute, Betsy Ferris Library Director, Sept. 18, 1997
[ii] Franklin Library Association - A Tribute, Betsy Ferris Library Director, Sept. 18, 1997
[iii] State Aid to Public Libraries, Mass. Board of Library Commissioners, 2017.
[iv] Annual Report, Town of Franklin, 1890. p. 26-27, 90-91.
[v] Seventy-Third Annual Report, Town of Franklin, For the Fiscal Year Ending December 31, 1930. p. 48-50.
[vi] Seventy-Sixth Annual Report of the Officers of the Town of Franklin for the Year Ending Dec. 31, 1933. p. 44-45. Dec. 31, 1933. p. 44-45.
[vii] Seventy-Ninth Annual Report of the Officers of the Town of Franklin, Massachusetts, For the Year Ending December 31st, 1936. p. 85-86.
[viii] Eighty-Sixth Annual Report of the Officers of the Town of Franklin for the Year Ending Dec. 31, 1943. p. 85.
[ix] Eighty-Eight Annual Report of the Officers of the Town of Franklin for the Year Ending Dec. 31, 1945. p. 49.
[x] Eighty-Ninth Annual Report of the Town of Franklin for the Year Ending Dec. 31, 1946. p. 33-34.
[xi] Ninetieth Annual Report of the Town of Franklin for the Year Ending Dec. 31, 1947. p. 32-33.
[xii] Ninety-Second Annual Report of the Town of Franklin for the Year Ending Dec. 31, 1949. p. 32-33.
[xiii] Ninety-Third Annual Report of the Officers of the Town of Franklin for the Year Ending Dec. 31, 1950. p. 37-38.
[xiv] Ninety-Fourth Annual Report of the Officers of the Town of Franklin for the Year Ending Dec. 31, 1951. p. 14-15.
[xv] Ninety-Fifth Annual Report of the Town of Franklin for the Year Ending Dec. 31, 1952. p. 14-15.
[xvi] Ninety-Sixth Annual Report, 1953. p. 30-31.
[xvii] Ninety-Seventh Annual Report of the Town of Franklin for the Year Ending Dec. 31, 1954. p. 45-46.
[xviii] Ninety-Eight Annual Report of the Officers of the Town of Franklin for the Fiscal Year Ending December 31, 1955. p. 45-46.
[xix] 1956: A pictorial presentation of Officials of your leading town departments, p. 35.
[xx] Annual Report, 1957. p. 36-37.
[xxi] One Hundred and Second Annual Report of the Officers of the Town of Franklin for the Year Ending December 31, 1959. p. 54.
[xxii] http://guides.mblc.state.ma.us/mblc-125-years/1955
[xxiii] http://guides.mblc.state.ma.us/mblc-125-years/1956
[xxiv] http://guides.mblc.state.ma.us/mblc-125-years/1960
[xxv] Franklin Annual Town Report, 1964. p. 136-137.
[xxvi] Franklin Annual Town Report, 1965. p. 119-120.

[xxvii] One Hundred and Ninth Annual Town Report, Franklin, Massachusetts, For the Year 1966. p. 100-101.
[xxviii] One Hundred and Tenth Annual Town Report, Franklin, Massachusetts, For the Year 1967. p. 93-94.
[xxix] Annual Report, Town of Franklin, 1968. p. 112-115.
[xxx] Annual Report, Town of Franklin, 1969. p. 224-226.
[xxxi] http://guides.mblc.state.ma.us/mblc-125-years/1972
[xxxii] Annual Report, Town of Franklin, 1971. p. 62-63.
[xxxiii] Annual Report, Town of Franklin, 1973. p. 60.
[xxxiv] Annual Report, Town of Franklin, 1974. p. 112-113.
[xxxv] Report for the Town of Franklin, January 1, 1979 through June 30, 1980. p. 142.
[xxxvi] Report for the Town of Franklin, July 1, 1981 through June 30, 1982. p. 25.
[xxxvii] Report for the Town of Franklin, July 1, 1982 through June 30, 1983. p. 3-4, 58-59.
[xxxviii] Franklin Town Report, 1983-1984. p. 62-63.
[xxxix] Franklin Annual Report, 1984-1985. p. 2-3.
[xl] Franklin Annual Report, 1985-1986. p. 26-28.
[xli] Franklin Annual Report, 1986-1987. p. 29-29.
[xlii] 1989, Annual Report, Town of Franklin. p. 128
[xliii] 1990, Annual Report, Town of Franklin. p. 41-42.
[xliv] 1991, Annual Report, Town of Franklin. p. 43.
[xlv] 1992, Annual Report, Town of Franklin. p. 40.
[xlvi] 1993, Annual Report, Town of Franklin. p. 36.
[xlvii] 1994, Annual Report, Town of Franklin. p. 41.
[xlviii] 1996, Annual Report, Town of Franklin. p. 30.
[xlix] 1997, Annual Report, Town of Franklin. p. 135.
[l] 1998, Annual Report, Town of Franklin. p. 150.